A

gift in memory

of

Dr. Edward F.P. Kearney

Storming to Power

By the Editors of Time-Life Books

Alexandria, Virginia

Time-Life Books Inc.
is a wholly owned subsidiary of

Time Incorporated

FOUNDER: Henry R. Luce 1898-1967
Editor-in-Chief: Jason McManus
Chairman and Chief Executive Officer:
J. Richard Munro
President and Chief Operating Officer:
N. J. Nicholas, Jr.
Editorial Director: Richard B. Stolley
Executive Vice President, Books: Kelso F. Sutton
Vice President, Books: Paul V. McLaughlin

Time-Life Books Inc.

EDITOR: George Constable
Executive Editor: Ellen Phillips
Director of Design: Louis Klein
Director of Editorial Resources: Phyllis K. Wise
Editorial Board: Russell B. Adams, Jr., Dale M.
Brown, Roberta Conlan, Thomas H. Flaherty, Lee
Hassig, Donia Ann Steele, Rosalind Stubenberg
Director of Photography and Research:
John Conrad Weiser
Assistant Director of Editorial Resources:
Elise Ritter Gibson

PRESIDENT: Christopher T. Linen
Chief Operating Officer: John M. Fahey, Jr.
Senior Vice Presidents: Robert M. DeSena,
James L. Mercer, Paul R. Stewart
Vice Presidents: Stephen L. Bair, Ralph J. Cuomo,
Neal Goff, Stephen L. Goldstein, Juanita T. James,
Carol Kaplan, Susan J. Maruyama, Robert H.
Smith, Joseph J. Ward
Director of Production Services:
Robert J. Passantino
Supervisor of Quality Control: James King

The Cover: On a rainy October day in 1930, Adolf
Hitler, leader of the fast-growing Nazi movement,
returns the salute of his marching Storm
Troopers during the annual party conclave in
the city of Weimar. That month, 107 Nazi
deputies took their seats in the Reichstag,
making the party the second largest in Germany.

This volume is one of a series that chronicles
the rise and eventual fall of Nazi Germany. Other
books in the series include:
The SS
Fists of Steel

The Third Reich

SERIES DIRECTOR: Thomas H. Flaherty
Series Administrator: Jane Edwin
Editorial Staff for *Storming to Power:*
Designer: Raymond Ripper
Picture Editor: Jane Coughran
Text Editors: John Newton, Henry Woodhead
Senior Writer: Stephen G. Hyslop
Researchers: Philip Brandt George, Jane A.
Martin (principal); Trudy Pearson
Assistant Designers: Alan Pitts, Tina Taylor
Copy Coordinator: Charles J. Hagner
Picture Coordinator: Robert H. Wooldridge, Jr.
Editorial Assistant: Patricia D. Whiteford

Special Contributors: Amy Aldrich, Ronald H.
Bailey, Donald Dale Jackson, Richard D. Kovar,
Thomas A. Lewis, Mayo Mohs, Brian C. Pohanka,
David S. Thomson (text); Marilyn Murphy, Philip
M. Murphy (research); Michael Kalen Smith
(index)

Editorial Operations
Copy Chief: Diane Ullius
Production: Celia Beattie
Library: Louise D. Forstall

Correspondents: Elisabeth Kraemer-Singh
(Bonn); Christine Hinze (London); Maria
Vincenza Aloisi (Paris); Ann Natanson (Rome).
Valuable assistance was also provided by:
Angelika Lemmer (Bonn); Elizabeth Brown,
Christina Lieberman (New York); Ann Wise
(Rome); Traudl Lessing (Vienna).

First printing. Printed in U.S.A.

Published simultaneously in Canada.
School and library distribution by Silver Burdett
Company, Morristown, New Jersey 07960.

TIME-LIFE is a trademark of Time Incorporated
U.S.A.

**Library of Congress Cataloging in
Publication Data**
Storming to power / by the editors of Time-Life
Books.
      p.   cm. — (The Third Reich)
   Bibliography: p.
   Includes index.
   ISBN 0-8094-6954-5.
   ISBN 0-8094-6955-3 (lib. bdg.)
   1. Germany—Politics and government—1918-
1933. 2. Hitler, Adolf, 1889-1945. 3. National-
sozialistische Deutsche Arbeitei-Partei—History.
I. Time-Life Books. II. Series.
DD240.S764 1989   943.085—dc19   88-24789

Other Publications:

AMERICAN COUNTRY
VOYAGE THROUGH THE UNIVERSE
THE TIME-LIFE GARDENER'S GUIDE
MYSTERIES OF THE UNKNOWN
TIME FRAME
FIX IT YOURSELF
FITNESS, HEALTH & NUTRITION
SUCCESSFUL PARENTING
HEALTHY HOME COOKING
UNDERSTANDING COMPUTERS
LIBRARY OF NATIONS
THE ENCHANTED WORLD
THE KODAK LIBRARY OF CREATIVE PHOTOGRAPHY
GREAT MEALS IN MINUTES
THE CIVIL WAR
PLANET EARTH
COLLECTOR'S LIBRARY OF THE CIVIL WAR
THE EPIC OF FLIGHT
THE GOOD COOK
WORLD WAR II
HOME REPAIR AND IMPROVEMENT
THE OLD WEST

For information on and a full description of any
of the Time-Life Books series listed above, please
call 1-800-621-7026 or write:
Reader Information
Time-Life Customer Service
P.O. Box C-32068
Richmond, Virginia 23261-2068

General Consultants

Col. John R. Elting, USA (Ret.), former asso-
ciate professor at West Point, has written or
edited some twenty books, including *Swords
around a Throne, The Superstrategists,* and
American Army Life, as well as *Battles for
Scandinavia* in the Time-Life Books World
War II series. He was chief consultant to the
Time-Life series, The Civil War.

William Sheridan Allen, is chairman of the
Department of History at the State University
of New York at Buffalo and the author of
numerous articles and books on the social
and political history of the Weimar Republic
and Nazi Germany, including *The Nazi Seizure of Power: The Experience of a Single
German Town.* He is also the editor and
translator of *The Infancy of Nazism: The
Memoirs of Ex-Gauleiter Albert Krebs, 1923-
1933,* and has written extensively on the anti-
Nazi underground.

Contents

Undeterred by the imprisonment of their leader, Adolf Hitler, uniformed Nazis flaunt the swastika at a right-wing rally in 1924.

The Politics of Hate

The warden of Landsberg prison delivered the news personally to the inmate in cell 7: He was to be paroled that very day, Saturday, December 20, 1924. Early in the afternoon, thirty-five-year-old Adolf Hitler gathered his belongings, including the unfinished manuscript of the book he was writing, shook hands with his jailers, and climbed into the back of a friend's touring car—a free man for the first time in more than a year.

Hitler soon was on his way home to Munich, scene of the abortive Beer Hall Putsch he had led in November 1923 in a bid to overthrow Germany's Weimar government. This ill-planned scheme had netted him a five-year sentence for treason and left his Nazi party officially outlawed. On Hitler's first day of freedom, a companion asked him what he would do now. "I shall start again," he replied, "from the beginning."

Both the condition of Hitler's party and the state of the German nation on that gray Bavarian afternoon gave his vow a hollow ring. He had built the National Socialist German Workers' party to a membership of 55,787 in the years before the putsch; now the party was all but moribund. Both it and its newspaper had been banned, Hitler had been prohibited from speaking in public, and he was in danger of being deported to his native Austria. Among his deputies, those who were not in exile or still imprisoned had formed rival factions and feuded bitterly over ideology. No serious contender had emerged to fill the void left by Hitler's arrest, and the leader himself had remained aloof from the bickering while enjoying a strikingly comfortable confinement at Landsberg. It appeared to many that the Nazi party was just another postwar fringe movement that had flickered fitfully for a year or two and then faded.

The country, too, had changed during the thirteen months since Hitler's arrest. The political and economic chaos that had marked the first few years of the Weimar Republic, creating an atmosphere of frustration and turmoil in which extremist groups flourished, had subsided. The ruinous inflation that had consumed the savings of millions of families was now under control; the currency was stable, and employment was on the rise. The crippling reparations payments imposed on Germany at the end of the

Paroled from Landsberg prison in December 1924, Adolf Hitler pauses for a photograph before boarding a friend's Maybach touring car for his return to Munich, headquarters of the Nazi party. Hitler had been jailed for his role in the 1923 Beer Hall Putsch and was released after serving thirteen months.

Great War had been reduced to a tolerable level. German industry was recovering with the aid of American loans. The adroit and persistent foreign minister, Gustav Stresemann, was pushing for the removal of the French troops occupying the Ruhr, a goal he would soon achieve. In Reichstag elections held the month Hitler was released, the moderate Social Democrats had improved their strength by 30 percent, while votes for right-wing racist factions and nationalist parties had declined by half. The Nazis had received only 3 percent of the ballots cast. Germany was calming down.

With his aim still firmly fixed on the overthrow of the republic, the ex-convict returned to his spartan apartment, where his neighbors had prepared a welcoming feast. Despite the disarray of the Nazi party and the unwelcome stability in the country, Hitler himself seemed more certain than ever of the zealot's vision that was his alone—that of a reborn and aggressive Reich entirely under his domination. The police knew what his release meant. "Hitler will, because of his energy, again become the driving force of new and serious public riots and a menace to the security of the state," a police report predicted. Hitler, in fact, was already planning his next revolutionary moves.

The calm that prevailed in Germany in 1924 would continue until the end of 1929, when the Great Depression would once again plunge the nation into social and economic turmoil. During the five quiet years, the firebrand whose coup attempt had fizzled would prudently bide his time and build a loyal organization. He would gather recruits, commit his political theories to paper in *Mein Kampf,* solidify his position as the party *Führer,* or leader, who was entitled to unquestioning obedience, and construct a political machine by emphasizing the twentieth-century art of propaganda.

After the depression changed conditions in Germany, Hitler would prove intimidating, ruthless, and violent, adept at dividing his political foes and exploiting a populace fearful of the future. What would remain consistent throughout his drive for dictatorial authority was his fanatical devotion to himself and his vision, a triumph of determination that would take him to the pinnacle of power. In August 1934, the final piece of the design that Hitler had refined in Landsberg prison would drop into place. In total victory, he would stand alone astride the German nation as both Reich chancellor and president.

It was at Landsberg, where he enjoyed such amenities as a cell with a handsome view, afternoons in the garden, and catered meals, that Hitler began writing the book he originally titled *Four and a Half Years of Struggle against Lies, Stupidity, and Cowardice.* Mercifully shortened to *Mein Kampf* (My struggle) by his publisher, the book was a sketchy review of his past and a rambling, overwrought, and often-tedious meditation on the future he envisioned for himself and Germany.

In both style and content, it was a book only a true believer could admire. Hitler's prose was ponderous and bombastic, the logic of his arguments, tortured. His "program" was mainly a list of what he opposed: Marxism, liberalism, parliamentary democracy, the educated middle class, capitalism, unions, the intelligentsia. He made no attempt to disguise his remedy for these evils—a racially pure state with himself as dictator and more *Lebensraum*, or living space, for Germans, gained largely at the expense of the Marxist Soviet Union.

A handbill for Hitler's autobiography uses his unwieldy title, *Four and a Half Years of Struggle against Lies, Stupidity, and Cowardice*, which was shortened to *Mein Kampf*, or my struggle.

Among the book's autobiographical passages were accounts of his early life in the city of Linz, Austria, and his years in Vienna as an orphaned teenager. The time he spent in Vienna, following the death of his mother late in 1907, was "the saddest period of my life," he wrote. He came to the capital from Linz at the age of eighteen, intending to study painting at the Academy of Fine Arts, but the school rejected him. He found work as a casual laborer—carrying bags, shoveling snow—and later as a painter of city scenes and posters, earning what he called "a truly meager living that never sufficed to appease even my daily hunger."

Citing his hunger and deprivation, he wrote, "I owe it to that period that I grew hard and am still capable of being hard." Although as an orphan Hitler received a small stipend from the government, the sum was hardly sufficient. He ate at soup kitchens and at times slept in doorways or flophouses. Those who knew the young Hitler were struck by his intense, opinionated personality and his odd blend of indolence—he avoided physical labor as much as possible—and lofty ambition. He neither smoked nor drank and often dressed in a long, seedy overcoat and wore a derby above his thin face and large penetrating eyes.

He read voraciously—anti-Semitic pamphlets, books on history, politics, and economics, and even volumes on mass psychology. He would later attribute his view of the world to his reading in Vienna; he declared with perverse pride that afterward he "had to learn little and to alter nothing." His Viennese interlude also served to introduce Hitler to "two menaces whose names I had previously scarcely known, and whose terrible im-

A Nazi truck rattles through the Brandenburg Gate during the 1924 campaign. Though officially banned, the Nazis worked with other right-wing parties to win thirty-two Reichstag seats.

portance for the existence of the German people I certainly did not understand: Marxism and Jewry."

Hitler's observation of Viennese politics, especially the workings of the dominant Social Democratic party, gave him insight into the techniques of propaganda and building a mass movement. The cynical conclusions he drew about molding the public mind would later prove astonishingly effective. Propaganda, he wrote, must be aimed at the lowest common denominator in the audience. A skilled propagandist knew a target's weaknesses. Emotional appeals were better than intellectual arguments. The

masses did not want freedom of choice, they wanted a simple doctrine and an enemy, and preferably just one enemy—dividing their hostility only confused them. Truth was irrelevant. Physical terror was a useful persuader. The way to deliver the message, whatever it was, was through public speaking: "The power that has always started the greatest religious and political avalanches in history has from time immemorial been the magic power of the spoken word, and that alone."

Hitler left Vienna in 1913, repelled by what he considered the city's poisonous racial mix, and moved to Munich—"a *German* city," he exulted, where he immediately felt at home. No longer the "half a boy" he had been when he came to Vienna, he was now a man, he wrote, "grown quiet and grave" at the age of twenty-four. When war broke out a year later, he eagerly enlisted in the German army and served as a courier for a unit that fought several engagements on the western front. A good soldier, though something of a loner, Hitler suffered a leg wound in 1916 and was temporarily blinded during a British gas attack a month before the armistice. He was in a hospital when Germany surrendered and the republic was created, acts he viewed as criminal betrayals of German honor. Demobilized a corporal, a proud wearer of the Iron Cross, First Class, he now decided on his life's work, politics.

In Munich, where the ambiance was friendly to right-wing movements, Hitler joined a minuscule political party—he was the fifty-fifth member—of like-minded anti-Semitic nationalists. He quickly discovered that he had a gift for speechmaking, and within months he was leading the infant National Socialist movement and practicing his talent for propaganda on Bavarian audiences. He easily beat back all challenges to his party leadership and encouraged the formation of a paramilitary squad of strong-armed thugs called the Sturmabteilung (SA), or Storm Troopers. The swastika became the party symbol. By mid-1923, the Nazis were publishing a daily newspaper, they had a vague program called the Twenty-five Points, and Hitler was gathering allies for the brazen coup he planned. The attempted putsch collapsed in a single burst of gunfire, but Hitler's eloquence at the ensuing trial made him a national name and a rightist hero. The former corporal had come a long way in four and a half years.

In his cell at Landsberg, Hitler mulled the lessons of the failed coup and plotted a new strategy. He concluded that sharing power was a mistake; he alone would henceforth give the orders because no one else could be trusted. He also recognized that it was not enough to oust an existing government; a revolutionary party must have a well-developed organizational structure of its own, a shadow cabinet, ready to supplant the fallen order. Hitler's third conclusion charted the party's course to power: The

Nazis would reject the tactic of an armed coup and follow a legal, constitutional route. "We shall have to hold our noses and enter the Reichstag against the Catholic and Marxist deputies," he told a prison visitor. "If outvoting them takes longer than outshooting them, at least the results will be guaranteed by their constitution." Once the Nazis gained a majority—as Hitler said they inevitably would—Germany would be theirs.

Two weeks after his release from Landsberg, Hitler met with the Bavarian prime minister Heinrich Held to assure the dubious minister that he had nothing to fear from the National Socialists, his loyal allies in the fight against communism. He asked Held to lift the prohibition that outlawed the party and banned his speeches, as well as the Nazi newspaper, the *Völkischer Beobachter*. Prompted by Justice Minister Franz Gürtner, a Nazi sympathizer, Held agreed in mid-February to remove the proscription. "The wild beast is checked," Held remarked to Gürtner with what proved to be more hope than accuracy. "We can afford to loosen the chain."

The Nazi paper that reappeared in Munich on February 26, 1925, carried an editorial by Hitler titled "A New Beginning." It called for squabbling party members to forget their differences and unite under his leadership in the struggle against Marxism and "its originators, the Jews." The next night he returned to the *Bürgerbräukeller*, scene of the maladroit putsch, to make his first public speech since his trial a year earlier.

Hitler's friends detected a change in his looks since his prison stint. He appeared stonier somehow, more severe. His face was "more forcefully composed," an acquaintance noticed, with "an unmistakable note of hardness." A cheering, rambunctious throng 4,000 strong filled the beer hall two hours before he was due to speak, and 1,000 more were turned away. Hitler's two-hour speech did not disappoint them.

Marxism would be vanquished, he cried, by "a doctrine of superior truthfulness, but the same brutality in execution." He alone would lead the movement, subject to no conditions "as long as I personally bear the responsibility." Several of his deputies leaped to their feet at the end of his passionate oration and rushed forward amid the bedlam to shake hands symbolically and pledge their loyalty. One disciple wrote that his doubts "melted away when the Führer spoke." Prior to this, Hitler had been called the Führer only in private; from now on his fellow Nazis would call him that in public, too.

But if the speech was a triumph of suasion, it was also a tactical blunder, for it alarmed the authorities whom Hitler had so recently taken pains to mollify. Hitler had clearly numbered the republican regime among the enemies of nazism. And to make it worse, the Führer, spurred by the crowd's wild excitement, had exclaimed that there were only two possible

Sitting under a laurel wreath, one of his favorite decorations, Hitler reads a newspaper in his cell.

A Term of Coddled Confinement

Hitler's jailers at Landsberg—many of them sympathetic to his cause —were so mesmerized by him that they made his term absurdly com-fortable. Lodged in a large, sunny cell, Hitler was allowed a daily stroll in the garden, all the books and newspapers he wanted, and many times the normal quota of visitors. He was exempted from manual la-bor; even the task of cleaning his quarters was done by a less privi-leged inmate. Food was plentiful and good—Hitler became paunchy in jail—and he was assigned a spe-cial table, where he chaired lunch-time meetings of imprisoned Nazis.

The high point of this cushy ex-istence came on Hitler's thirty-fifth birthday, when so many cakes, strudels, flowers, and other gifts flowed in from the party faithful that the warden set aside several rooms to cope with the overflow.

The Bavarian sun streams through the wide windows of Hitler's top-floor cell. The pampered Nazis, complained a Landsberg inmate, "were not equal before the law, nor were they equal as prisoners."

Hitler is joined in his cell by fellow Nazis jailed for their parts in the beer-hall fiasco. They include Hitler's chauffeur, Emil Maurice *(holding a mandolin),* and his secretary, Rudolf Hess *(second from right).* The picture was taken with a camera that had been smuggled into the prison by Hess's fiancée.

A one-time fortress, Landsberg prison sits on a hill, its gray-white cellblocks enclosed by stone walls twenty feet high. Hitler was held in a block reserved for political prisoners.

ends to the Nazi struggle—"either the enemy passes over our bodies or we pass over theirs." This was too much for the Bavarian government, which ten days later once again forbade Hitler to speak in public, although the ban stopped short of outlawing either the party or its newspaper. The Bavarian prohibition would remain in effect for two years. All but four of the other seventeen German states likewise barred Hitler from the public podiums he sought as the essential springboards to power. These obstacles would not prove insurmountable, however.

In the years before the Beer Hall Putsch, Hitler had welcomed as comrades in the movement Erich Ludendorff, the powerful quartermaster general of the German army during World War I, and Ernst Röhm, commander of a paramilitary organization called the *Frontbann,* or Front Liners. Hitler afforded the two men the status of allies who retained their own bases of power in the Nazi party. But the reborn party had room at the top for only one. Hitler broke with Ludendorff after the presidential election of March 1925, in which Ludendorff made a pathetic showing as the Nazi candidate, winning just 211,000 of 27 million votes cast. By this time, Röhm had helped to found another quasi-military organization, the SA. This gang of ex-soldiers and roughnecks was originally formed to keep order at party meetings and protect party leaders, but before long they were brawling in the streets with rival political factions.

Hitler and Röhm quarreled repeatedly about the role of the brown-shirted Storm Troopers and who should control them. Röhm insisted that his men remain independent of the party structure and that he stay at the helm. Hitler, who believed the SA owed its first loyalty to the party and the Führer, rejected Röhm's demand outright. Röhm submitted his resignation and asked for an acknowledgment. Receiving no reply, he wrote again, reminding Hitler of their comradeship before the putsch and pleading not to be denied "your personal friendship." When this entreaty brought no response, he announced his resignation, which received only a brief notice in the party paper. He grumbled to a friend that Hitler had "adorned himself with borrowed plumage" by appropriating the SA. Disillusioned, Röhm went to Bolivia as a military instructor, but Hitler would eventually summon him back.

Gregor Strasser, a beefy, easygoing Bavarian druggist, was another ambitious party member. A deputy in the Reichstag, he had made himself indispensable by developing a network of contacts in northern Germany,

In exile during the late 1920s after a quarrel with Hitler, SA chief Ernst Röhm wears a Bolivian army uniform. The bridge of Röhm's nose had been shot away during World War I.

Powerfully built Gregor Strasser stands bareheaded at the center of a group of Nazis he organized in northern Germany. On Strasser's left, in dark uniform and glasses, stands his secretary, Heinrich Himmler.

where he had campaigned while Hitler was in Landsberg. Declaring himself a "colleague," not a "follower," Strasser was disinclined to grant Hitler the absolute fealty he demanded. In fact, he would later become Hitler's only real challenger for party leadership. But for the moment, he was content to accept the Führer's wily offer to take charge of the party organization in the north. This move gave Strasser independence, got him out of Hitler's way, and delayed the inevitable confrontation between the two.

The order forbidding Hitler to speak in public, which among other effects deprived him of his main source of income, did not daunt him. He needed to work behind the scenes to build a top-to-bottom party organization anyway, and the timing of the ban was propitious for him: Germany, for the moment, remained tranquil and relatively prosperous and thus hostile to the oratorical entreaties of extremists. The ban did not prevent his addressing groups of forty or fifty at private homes, as he did frequently, and he picked up the slack in his income by collecting fees for his articles in the party press. He traveled the country speaking at closed-door organizational meetings, where he also nurtured the personality cult he was carefully creating. In April 1925, he finessed the threat of deportation by going to Linz, Austria, his birthplace, and asking that his citizenship be

Beneath smoking urns, top-hatted Berliners attend the transfer of Friedrich Ebert's coffin to its resting place in Heidelberg. The Weimar president's sudden death opened the way for a fiercely contested election in 1925.

voided. Since he was a German resident and a veteran of the German army, Austrian officials promptly acceded. As a result, Hitler was technically a man without a country until a pro-Nazi minister of the state of Braunschweig granted him German citizenship in 1932.

Meanwhile, the sudden death of President Friedrich Ebert in February 1925 had precipitated an election that exposed sharp divisions in the electorate. Ebert, who died of appendicitis at the age of fifty-four, was a Social Democrat who had skillfully maneuvered the republic through its shaky beginnings. The seven candidates who ran to succeed him spanned the Weimar spectrum from the Communist Ernst Thälmann on the left to the Nazi Ludendorff on the right. The three leading contenders for the seven-year term were Otto Braun of the Social Democrats, Wilhelm Marx of the Center party, and Karl Jarres of the Nationalists, all of whom were generally conservative and opposed to the republic. In the March election, Jarres finished first and Braun second, but since no candidate won a majority, another election was necessary.

In the subsequent contest, the Nationalists, now backed by the Nazis, abandoned Jarres and shrewdly turned to a seventy-eight-year-old war hero, Paul von Hindenburg, perhaps the most revered figure in the country. The prorepublic factions—the Center party and the Social Democrats —united behind Marx. Hindenburg won by a margin of 3.3 percent, in part because many republican factions deserted Marx at the last minute in favor of his opponent. The elderly field marshal, a monarchist all his life, confessed that he felt uncomfortable presiding over a government alien to his beliefs, but he promised to respect the democratic constitution regardless. In fact, his victory had the ironic effect of reconciling many antidemocratic Germans to the Weimar regime.

Foreign Minister Stresemann, worried about the Allies' reaction to the election of a war hero and monarchist as German president, was nonetheless able to negotiate the evacuation of French troops from the Ruhr in August of 1925. He also enhanced Germany's international stature by playing a major role in the creation of the Locarno Pact, a series of agreements signed later in the year that guaranteed the borders of Germany, France, and Belgium.

Hitler lived at this time in a two-room, linoleum-floored flat in a working-class section of Munich, but he frequently left these humble surroundings and traveled to the Bavarian Alps. In the spectacular mountains near the Alpine village of Berchtesgaden, he finished dictating the first volume of *Mein Kampf* in the summer of 1925 and immediately commenced work on volume two, which appeared in late 1926. He supported himself on book royalties (in 1925, 9,473 copies were sold; the following year, 6,913), fees for articles, gifts from well-to-do supporters, and whatever he kept from the contributions that flowed into the party treasury. When income-tax officials questioned him—he identified himself as a writer on his tax return—he pleaded poverty. "Nowhere do I possess property or other capital assets that I can call my own," he told them. "I restrict of necessity my personal wants and take my meals in modest restaurants." The tax investigators were especially interested in his expensive red Mercedes six-seater, which was never without a chauffeur because Hitler did not drive. Hitler protested that the luxury car was "but a means to an end" and that it enabled him "to accomplish my daily work." He had liked fast cars all his life; on the day he left prison, he had asked the man driving him to Munich from Landsberg to accelerate, but the driver had replied, "No, it's my firm intention to go on living another twenty-five years."

On his visits to the mountains, Hitler donned lederhosen and walked in the forests. ("Having to change into long trousers was always a misery to me," he wrote.) Sometimes he would stay away from Munich for several weeks, suring only to issue an order or a reprimand to the party faithful. He eventually rented a handsome wooden villa near Berchtesgaden called Haus Wachenfeld, which he furnished with the help of wealthy friends—among them, relatives of the composer Richard Wagner.

Ill at ease in most social situations, Hitler rejected a suggestion that he learn to waltz. Dancing was "too effeminate," he said. He also declined to swim, declaring that politicians should not be photographed in swim trunks. He was similarly averse to suggestions that he travel to the United States or Asia or study another language. "What do you think I can learn from them?" he demanded.

At Berchtesgaden, Hitler fell in love. He met a shopgirl named Mitzi Reiter while they were walking their dogs in the local park. The girl's older sister objected to his approaches because of the difference in their ages: Reiter was only sixteen years old, and Hitler was thirty-six. But he persisted. He invited the sisters to a Nazi party meeting, charmed them, and soon was accompanying the young Reiter on frequent outings. Early in their relationship, according to Reiter, Hitler stopped in a secluded spot on one of their walks and suddenly kissed her. "He said, 'I want to crush you,'" she recalled. "He was full of wild passion." She dreamed of marriage, but Hitler did not, and after about two years of intermittent liaisons in Berchtesgaden and Munich, Reiter attempted to strangle herself with a piece of clothesline hung from a doorknob. Her brother discovered her as she lay unconscious, and he saved her life.

Hitler's extended sojourns in the mountains in mid-1925 may have distracted him from a challenge to his authority that rapidly grew into open revolt. The rebel leader was Gregor Strasser, the genial and unintimidated overseer of Nazi efforts in northern Germany. Strasser had established a daily newspaper in Berlin and built a following as a hardworking and effective organizer who sympathized with the downtrodden. To Hitler's dismay, Strasser took the word *socialism* in National Socialism seriously; he wanted to identify the party with the German proletariat—while rejecting international communism. His chief ally in this deviation from the Führer's chosen path was a well-educated, jockey-size Rhinelander who was just coming into his own as a Nazi luminary—Paul Joseph Goebbels.

Goebbels was complex, politically and personally. His Catholic parents had wanted him to be a priest. As a child, he had been stricken with an ailment that left one of his legs withered and shorter than the other. A bright student but considered arrogant by his schoolmates, he aspired to be a writer and had attended eight different universities before taking a Ph.D. in literature at Heidelberg. In his twenties, he wrote a romantic autobiographical novel that was not published, as well as several plays that

Foreign Minister Gustav
Stresemann jokes with newsmen
in Locarno, Switzerland, on
October 16, 1925, after signing
a protocol guaranteeing the
shrunken borders fixed for
his nation by the Versailles
treaty. The Locarno Pact led
to Germany's acceptance
into the League of Nations.

never saw production; Goebbels had also failed to find work in journalism.

He joined the party in 1924, when he was twenty-seven years old, and quickly found his niche as a speaker and writer, with a feel for propaganda that rivaled Hitler's. Strasser, impressed by Goebbels's speaking ability, hired him as his secretary, and Goebbels became editor of a biweekly newsletter for party leaders. Like Strasser, Goebbels was sympathetic to socialist goals and believed that the Nazis should represent workers and unions, despite Hitler's shrill antilabor imprecations in *Mein Kampf.* He even suggested that nazism and communism might somehow unite in German nationalism, publicly assuring a German communist that they were "not really enemies."

Strasser and Goebbels complained about how Nazi power was concentrated in the hands of "the calcified big shots in Munich." They also wanted more ideological content in what passed for the party program, the collection of anti-Semitic and vague semisocialist pronouncements in the Twenty-five Points of 1920. Specifically, they wanted more emphasis on such socialist aims as public ownership of industries and large estates. Strasser, whose conception of socialism was fuzzy at best, felt that the party's doctrine was more important than its leader. This alone was enough to set him on a collision course with Hitler.

The would-be rebellion began quietly in the late summer of 1925 at meetings of the northern gauleiters, or regional party leaders. Careful not to criticize the Führer directly (except for muttered asides about "the pope in Munich"), the gauleiters set up a committee headed by Strasser to draft a new program. Strasser's position was delicate. If he was out to dislodge Hitler, as he may have been, he kept quiet about it. Frequently disagreeing with one another, the conspirators drew up a revised program that differed from the Twenty-five Points more in emphasis than in overall direction. It repeated the anti-Semitic demands (deportation of recent Jewish immigrants, stripping other Jews of German citizenship) and expanded and clarified the economic sections. Strasser circulated the document among the northern leaders but said nothing to Munich about it.

The emergence of a new national issue—a demand by left-wing parties that the state dispossess deposed German royal families of money and property—brought the revolt within the party to a head. Strasser and Goebbels backed the idea and thought that the Nazis should support it as a show of solidarity with the proletariat. The notion was anathema to Hitler, who was courting conservatives by portraying himself as a steadfast anti-communist and staunch defender of private property. He lambasted the demand for expropriation as a Jewish swindle, but his opposition was primarily practical. With an open break in the Nazi party now seemingly inevitable, Strasser summoned the northern gauleiters to a showdown meeting in Hanover on November 22, 1925.

Goebbels created a stir at the outset by demanding the ejection of Hitler's representative, economic theorist Gottfried Feder, on grounds that he was a "stool pigeon" for the Führer, but the twenty-five-man group voted narrowly to let Feder stay. In addition to other differences, the meeting exposed a breach in the party line on the question of foreign policy. Goebbels and others urged an alliance with the Soviet Union against the "Jewish-capitalist West," disputing those who shared Hitler's opinion that Russia blocked German expansion. Goebbels, in fact, turned out to be the most visible and vociferous person attending the meeting. When Feder protested that such radical shifts in party policy were out of order in the Führer's absence, Goebbels, according to one participant, leaped to his feet and shouted, "In these circumstances, I demand that the petit bourgeois Adolf Hitler be expelled from the National Socialist party!" The quiet rebellion was quiet no longer.

In lederhosen and a Bavarian jacket, Hitler vacations near Berchtesgaden in the late 1920s. Even before he bought an Alpine retreat, Hitler relaxed in style, thanks to the generosity of a widow who rented her villa for a hundred reichsmarks (about twenty-seven dollars) per month.

With only two dissenting votes, the Hanover rebels endorsed governmental seizure of royal property. They went on to approve Strasser's revised program by the same lopsided margin. Strasser, perhaps emboldened by this heady show of defiance, took it a step further: He rejected Hitler's strategy of constitutional legality in favor of what he termed the "politics of catastrophe," a return to the revolutionary militance that had led to the putsch. This proposal, however, did not come to a vote. Feder hurried back to Munich to report to the Führer on the developments at Hanover.

Hitler had remained silent on the northern defection thus far, but the rebels had now forced his hand. He put little stock in party programs. To him the issue was, as always, himself: The party's policy was what the Führer said it was, no more and no less. To defy any part of his program for any reason amounted to treason against both nazism and himself as its incarnation. He determined to stress this in no uncertain terms to his followers at a meeting of party leaders at Bamberg, in southern Germany, on February 14, 1926.

Hitler carefully stage-managed the confrontation. He packed the hall with loyal gauleiters from the south and saw that banners and posters were hung throughout the town. He arrived escorted by a fleet of cars, like a head of state. Ascending the podium, he spoke for four hours, never attacking Strasser or Goebbels directly but repudiating point by point every subversive stand they had taken: The twenty-five-point program was sacrosanct —men had died for it. Expropriation was wrong because the party stood for private property. Russia was Germany's enemy. The legal path to power was tactically superior to revolution. After Hitler had concluded in a crescendo of bombast, a tepid thirty-minute debate followed. "Strasser speaks," Goebbels wrote in his diary that night. "Hesitant, trembling, clumsy, good, honest Strasser. Lord, what a poor match we are for those pigs down there!" Goebbels himself had been stunned into silence. Hitler draped a patronizing arm around Strasser and expansively told him to use party funds "to set yourself up properly as a man of your worth should." Hitler again reigned unchallenged. At the Führer's request, Strasser asked his co-conspirators to return the draft program he had circulated. And Hitler henceforth forbade "working groups" such as Strasser's original cell.

For the time being, Strasser remained a loyal Nazi, but Hitler never succeeded in totally subjugating him. Not so with Goebbels. Within a few weeks, he underwent a remarkable transformation and became Hitler's most ardent acolyte. Goebbels had been crushed by the defeat at Bamberg; strangely, he reacted as though his rival, Hitler, had betrayed him. "My heart aches," he lamented. "One of my greatest disappointments. I can no longer wholly believe in Hitler. This is terrible. I have lost my inner support." But the Führer wooed him with flattery and attention—asking him to speak in Munich, offering his car, phoning him personally, inviting him to Berchtesgaden. "I love him," Goebbels confessed to his diary in April. "I bow to the political genius." Goebbels was clever enough to hitch himself to the lone star in the Nazi firmament. "With him you can conquer the world," he gushed. "I am his to the end."

The referendum that would have allowed the German government to confiscate royal property failed in a nationwide plebiscite in June. Thus Goebbels's reversal of allegiance was further confirmed. Two months later, he publicly broke with Strasser and his northern colleagues. "Don't talk so much about ideals," he scolded them in an open letter. The Führer "is the instrument of the divine will."

Hitler followed his triumph at Bamberg with moves designed to consolidate his hold over every facet of nazism. He created a party judicial system known by its acronym, USCHLA, to preserve discipline and tighten control by quietly settling intraparty squabbles and imposing penalties. The first chief of this tribunal mistakenly thought his job was to punish corruption rather than to uphold discipline as the Führer defined it; he was quickly replaced by a more easily managed appointee.

With internal harmony restored, the Nazis staged their first Party Day rally in three years at Weimar on July 3 and 4, 1926. Weimar appealed to Hitler as a location for the event because the republic he was determined to destroy had been born there seven years earlier. Perhaps more important, Weimar was in Thuringia, one of the few states that allowed Hitler to speak in public. His guidelines for the meeting at Weimar stressed that

The map shows central Europe with the following labeled features:

Bodies of water and seas: NORTH SEA, BALTIC SEA

Countries: DENMARK, SWEDEN, LITHUANIA, NETHERLANDS, BELGIUM, FRANCE, SWITZERLAND, POLAND, CZECHOSLOVAKIA, AUSTRIA, HUNGARY, LUX. (Luxembourg)

German states/regions: PRUSSIA, EAST PRUSSIA, POLISH CORRIDOR, OLDENBURG, LÜBECK, HAMBURG, BREMEN, MECKLENBURG-STRELITZ, MECKLENBURG-SCHWERIN, SCHAUMBURG-LIPPE, LIPPE, BRAUNSCHWEIG, ANHALT, THURINGIA, WALDECK, SAXONY, HESSE, BAVARIA, WÜRTTEMBERG, BADEN, SAAR, EUPEN-MALMÉDY, ALSACE-LORRAINE, NORTH SCHLESWIG, ALPS

Cities: Copenhagen, Königsberg, Danzig, Kiel, Altona, Hamburg, Amsterdam, Leiden, The Hague, Hanover, Potsdam, Berlin, Neukölln, Schöneberg, Bad Harzburg, Detmold, Braunschweig, Halle, Leipzig, Düsseldorf, Cologne, Weimar, Brussels, Warsaw, Frankfurt, Bamberg, Prague, Luxembourg, Mannheim, Heidelberg, Nuremberg, Munich, Linz, Vienna, Budapest, Bad Wiessee, Berchtesgaden, Basel, Bern

Rivers: Elbe River, Oder River, Vistula River, Bug River, Rhine River, Ruhr River, Spree River, Danube River

The Weimar Republic—named for the city in central Germany where its constitution was written in 1919—was a bewildering patchwork of federated states, dominated by Prussia in the north and Bavaria in the south. Hitler viewed such internal divisions as threats to the nation's recovery as a great power; he called for a united Reich, where the Nazis could work their will "on the whole German nation, without consideration of previous federated-state boundaries." Once that goal was achieved, Hitler would turn his attention to Germany's neighbors and seek to "secure for the German people the land and the soil to which they are entitled."

debates were out of order. The only motions on the table were those already approved. The purpose of the event was to give "new incentive to the movement." There would be no echoes of Hanover.

Participants received a minute-by-minute schedule and detailed instructions—obey the police, do not smoke in meeting halls and sleeping quarters, purchase a Party Day badge for fifty pfennigs. On the first morning, a special train from Bavaria disgorged 2,000 loyalists clad in lederhosen. They marched through the streets to the music of martial bands. After reveille at six the next morning, there was a consecration of SA units' flags. This was followed by meetings and speeches, all leading to the main event, Hitler's address on "politics, ideas, and organization." The speech was a rambling screed. It denounced Germany's pallid role on the world stage and exalted the racial state that would restore Germanic pride. The treaties signed by the Weimar regime, he declared, were "null and void for us." When Hitler finished, 5,000 marchers paraded by in review, and for the first time the Führer and his troops exchanged the rigid-arm salute borrowed from the Italian Fascists.

Reaction to the weekend rally in the non-Nazi press ranged from indifference to scorn. Newspaper reports that the delegates brawled in cafés and molested citizens prompted the Nazi party paper to blast "Jewish-controlled" news organs. But Hitler was not overly concerned with criticism from outside the party. He sensed that the future of the movement he had spawned rested entirely on his powers of persuasion. And in the belief that the spoken word was his main weapon, the Führer had honed his oratorical skills, developing two contrasting and equally effective speaking styles. When addressing the faithful, he was passionate, theatrical, and vehement, a hot-eyed podium pounder who at times seemed on the verge of losing control. But when speaking to the uninitiated, he looked and sounded quite reasonable and thus was more persuasive. In a speech to a private group in Hamburg in early 1926, for example, he calmly built a case for the Nazi way not on racism but on patriotism, relying more on logic than emotion. When he finished, the conservative crowd gave him a rousing ovation.

His speeches appeared extemporaneous, but in fact he crafted them carefully, jotting key phrases and lines on notepaper. He choreographed his podium gestures under the tutelage of an astrologer who was an expert in body language. Hitler drank as many as twenty small bottles of mineral water during a speech and sometimes kept ice on the rostrum to cool his

His mouth sealed with tape that reads "speech ban," Hitler glares from a 1926 cartoon. In the address that caused the Bavarian government to silence him, Hitler said his Nazis would fight "not according to middle-class standards, but over corpses!"

REDE VERBOT
REDE VERBOT

hands. Many of his techniques became dogma when the party established a school for public speaking late in 1926.

Between public appearances, Hitler concentrated on the party's internal problems. The freewheeling Storm Troopers asserted their independence, refusing to acknowledge the party's ultimate authority. Shortly after the Weimar rally, the Führer moved to rein them in by selecting a seemingly more tractable SA commander to replace the disaffected Ernst Röhm. Hitler named Franz Pfeffer von Salomon, a former army captain, the new chief and ordered him to deemphasize the military character of the Brownshirts in favor of sports, propaganda, and mass intimidation. Boxing and jujitsu would supplant rifle practice. The SA would show the Marxists through mass marches that "National Socialism is the future master of the streets."

But Pfeffer proved less malleable than the Führer had anticipated. The new commander and the war veterans who made up most of the SA force never abandoned the flinty military stance they had displayed under Röhm. While they marched and saluted in the service of nazism, they continued to consider themselves equal if not superior to the party's civilian branch, and they defied all efforts to bring them to heel. Pfeffer's main contribution, meanwhile, was the blizzard of administrative acronyms—SABE, GRUSA, BEZ, GRUF—that filled his organizational charts.

Hitler was more successful in his attempt to subdue another pocket of chronic resistance to his hegemony, the unruly and faction-torn party organization in "Red Berlin." The Nazi gau, or district, in Berlin numbered only about 1,000 members, and in the contest for recruits it came in a sorry third to the better-organized Socialists and Communists. Gau meetings were so raucous and ineffectual that some members asked Hitler to name a new gauleiter. His inspired choice, in November 1926, was the fast-rising master of propaganda, Joseph Goebbels.

Goebbels whipped Berlin into line within weeks. He asserted his command so forcefully that 200 members quit on the spot, a price he was willing to pay. He straightened out party finances and held mass meetings. He alone among the gauleiters had been authorized by Hitler to use SA detachments, and he sent the Storm Troopers into the streets to cruise for fights with the Communists. The result was a strong and unified Nazi cell.

Placing Goebbels in Berlin served another useful purpose for Hitler—to humble Strasser. The liberal slant of Strasser's party newspaper in Berlin rankled Goebbels. For his part, Strasser regarded Goebbels as a traitor for his defection to the Führer. As the enmity between the two top Nazis in Berlin grew stronger, Goebbels bought his own journal, called *Der Angriff* (The assault), and directed it against Strasser. Goebbels also employed physical tactics, sending his SA toughs to beat up Strasser's followers.

When Strasser complained to Hitler, the Führer professed helplessness.

Goebbels, the man whom Berlin Nazis called "our doctor," had a genius for creating confrontations. He scheduled one mass meeting in a hall where Communists often met and loaded the room with Storm Troopers in anticipation of a brawl. When a free-for-all erupted, Nazi toughs in a balcony bombarded the outnumbered Communists with chairs, bottles, and beer mugs. In the days following this display of brute strength, some 2,600 applications for membership poured into Nazi headquarters.

At another meeting, however, Goebbels tried the patience of the Berlin authorities once too often. When a heckler interrupted the proceedings, Goebbels had his SA toughs beat up the man and throw him out of the hall. As it happened, the offender was an elderly former minister, and his treatment by the Nazis triggered a public uproar. Soon after the incident, the police chief prohibited local party activities. Although the ban would last eleven months, Goebbels quickly found a way around it; he disguised the party meetings with cover names such as the Funny-Money Savings Club, the Strike Bowling Society, and the High-Wave Swimming Club.

Goebbels's confrontational tactics in Berlin reflected an implicit decision by Hitler to redirect his recruitment efforts. To attract great numbers, Hitler had to woo the German middle class, which was indeed a fertile field: Fearful of the laboring class and the threat of communism, suspicious of the republican government and the moneyed elite, the members of the middle class were the natural receptors of Hitler's message of hate and empowerment. But now the Führer saw an opportunity to compete with the Communist party for the workers of Germany's big industrial cities. The new tactic, in effect, endorsed the leftward swing Strasser and Goebbels had urged. For the time being at least, Hitler viewed this Urban Plan as a promising avenue to Nazi growth and glory, even if it meant vying with the Marxists in anticapitalist rhetoric and alarming the well-to-do. The Führer's ideology, as always, was flexible: If the votes were in the Red cities, he would color National Socialism red. The Nazis would ascend to power, Goebbels wrote, "by developing two dozen cities into unshakable foundations of our movement." The key ingredients, as he demonstrated in Berlin, were strong local organizations and SA rule in the streets.

On March 5, 1927, two years after barring Hitler from speaking in public, Bavaria again lifted the ban in exchange for his vow to obey the laws. Four days later, he returned to Munich's Zirkus Krone, site of many earlier oratorical triumphs, to deliver another stemwinder before a crowd of 7,000.

The scene was a pageant, bursting with pomp and fervor, meticulously planned, and carefully choreographed to milk the audience of all its emo-

The first issue of the Nazi newspaper *Der Angriff* (The assault), published in Berlin on July 4, 1927, by Joseph Goebbels *(far right)*, featured a shrill warning of a communist putsch and a caricature of Jakob Goldschmidt, a Jewish banker *(lower left)*.

tion and some of its money. According to a police report of the event, "There is a craving for sensation in the hot air. The band plays rousing marches while fresh crowds keep pouring in. The *Völkischer Beobachter* is hawked about the grounds. At the ticket office each visitor is given a program of the National Socialist German Workers' party, and at the entrance a slip is pressed into everyone's hand warning against provocations and emphasizing the need to maintain order. Small flags are sold: 'Welcoming flags, ten pfennigs apiece.' They are either black, white, and red or entirely red, and show the swastika. The women are the best customers."

When Hitler entered, the audience roared a welcoming "Heil!" People stood on the benches, cheered, and stamped their feet as the Führer made his way to the stage with his retinue. A trumpet blast silenced the throng and signaled a procession of Storm Troopers, led by drummers and accompanied by flags—"glittering standards with swastikas inside a wreath and with eagles, modeled after the ancient Roman military standards."

As the troopers stood at attention, Hitler stepped to the front of the stage. "He speaks without a manuscript, at first in a slow, emphatic way," the police report continued. "Later, the words come tumbling forth, and in passages spoken with exaggerated emotion, his voice becomes thin and high and ceases to be intelligible. He gestures with arms and hands, jumps agitatedly about, and is bent on fascinating the thousands in the audience, who listen with close attention. When applause interrupts him, he raises his hands theatrically."

The combination of showmanship and tight discipline that now characterized the Nazi campaign was also displayed five months later at a rally that launched a new series of annual *Parteitage*, or Party Days, in the handsome old imperial city of Nuremberg. On this occasion, forty-seven special trains delivered Storm Troopers, members of the newly formed Hitler Youth, outlawed Berlin Nazis, and other delegates. A newspaper reporter observed that most of the arrivals seemed to be "young office clerks and students." They assembled outside the city on a large field where Count Zeppelin had once landed a dirigible. On the third day of the rally, more than 15,000 SA men, marching in regiments and battalions, each with its own flag and band, paraded with Adolf Hitler in the vanguard.

Nazi speakers at Nuremberg lamented the shortage of funds in party coffers—Hitler himself passed his hat in the audience—and approved a proposal to create a scientific association in hopes of attracting intellectuals to the party. Hitler's speech emphasized lebensraum and the failings of government based on majority rule. Artur Dinter, the gauleiter of Thuringia, presented the first systematic set of prospective anti-Semitic statutes, precursors of the Nuremberg Laws of 1935: Judaism would be illegal;

Jews would be barred from German citizenship and forbidden to teach, own property, or marry Aryans; Jews who had intimate relations with non-Jews would be hanged. It was an ugly omen of what lay ahead.

Hitler's public appearances in 1927 marked the end of a period of formidable achievement for him. During most of nazism's low-profile years, he had been barred from public platforms. Consequently, he had been free to concentrate on the pragmatic demands of building membership and fashioning a strong organization. In April of 1925, he could count on a hard core of 521 men. By December of that year, the party rolls had swelled to roughly 50,000. By 1928, enrollment had reached 75,000, and by the following year, 100,000. The party faithful were likely to be small-business people and merchants, artisans, white-collar workers, lower-level civil servants, and students. When farmers began feeling financially pinched in 1928, they became another important pool of Nazi support.

The Führer, of course, stood in solitary splendor atop the party apparatus. A *Reichsleitung*, or party directorate, occupied the next rung down. It consisted of a secretary, treasurer, and secretary general. Then came the government-in-waiting, evidence of Hitler's belief that a "new state" must be ready when the old one failed: quasi ministries of justice, foreign affairs, economics, agriculture, interior, science, labor, the press, industry, race and culture, and propaganda.

The gaus, or districts, formed the heart of the party structure. Gauleiters were required to submit a monthly progress report to Munich headquarters, but for the most part they ran their gaus without interference from higher up. Hitler chose his district leaders with great care. He selected efficient, hardworking, loyal men and was quick to replace any who failed to measure up. Consequently, the gaus practically ran themselves, freeing Hitler to concentrate on party strategy and other long-range matters.

Town or village units, each with a minimum of about fifteen members, answered to the gau. The local groups frequently came together in district meetings that featured a stirring guest speaker, chosen for the occasion from a list of approved orators compiled and maintained by party headquarters. Such speakers skillfully wove local issues into their appeals for nazism and custom-tailored their words to suit the evening's audience. For example, in a heavily Lutheran area, the message might bear an anti-Catholic bias, and vice versa.

Such gatherings provided most of the funds needed to operate the party in the early years. Not only was admission charged, but the hat was passed during the evening, and the donations usually matched the admission receipts. The gaus also maintained shops that raised money by selling Nazi insignia, uniforms, and pamphlets. Sums from these grass-roots sources far

As members of an enthusiastic crowd join in, Hitler salutes the parade concluding the 1927 party rally in Nuremberg. Saluting

from the running board of the Führer's flower-strewn Mercedes is Franz Pfeffer von Salomon, recently named chief of the SA.

surpassed money from the pockets of the rich conservatives whom Hitler courted during the party's formative period.

Hitler made the party attractive by creating a raft of auxiliaries that catered to special groups: Hitler Youth and the Nazi German Student League, the Teachers' League, Law Officers' League, and Physicians' League; gardeners and even poultry farmers had their own auxiliaries. A Nazi women's league was formed in 1928.

Gregor Strasser, erstwhile leader of the Hanover dissidents and still an important man in the party, was named chief political organizer in January 1928. Strasser's attitude toward Hitler seemed to be coming around to an acceptably reverent stance: "The sincerest devotion to the idea of National Socialism," he wrote, "is bound up with a deep love of the person of our Führer." Goebbels, who had professed his devotion earlier, was named director of propaganda.

Another man destined to emerge as a prominent Hitler deputy had come home to Germany after a four-year exile. Hermann Göring, the World War I flying ace, had fled the country after the 1923 putsch and spent most of the intervening years in Sweden, where he married the daughter of a baron. Still a fervent Nazi, he was Hitler's link to the moneyed class. After returning to Berlin at the end of 1927, he had become a consultant to Lufthansa, the German national airline, and renewed the friendships he had made among the royal family and the titans of industry. Hitler tapped Göring, along with Goebbels, Strasser, and others, to run in the 1928 Reichstag elections.

By early 1928, it had become clear that Hitler's plan to recruit industrial workers in Germany's big cities had foundered: The working classes remained loyal to the Socialists and Communists. Since the Urban Plan had never been formally announced, there was no need to renounce it. The plan simply tailed off. Hitler indirectly acknowledged the change in tactics in April when he replied to critics who had lumped the Nazis with left-wing radicals. As though the case had never been otherwise, he restated his loyalty to private property—with the exception of Jewish private property. Nazi recruiters henceforth resumed cultivation of the middle class—their natural constituency—and paid more attention to wooing the farmers.

The May election returns were a setback for the Nazis and other parties on the far right. Hitler himself, still stateless after giving up his Austrian citizenship, could not run. But his nominees, identified on the ballot as Hitler Movement candidates, polled only 810,000 of the 31 million votes cast and won just 12 of the Reichstag's 491 seats. The right-wing Nationalists lost 30 seats, and the Social Democrats gained 21; the Nazis stood as the ninth-ranking party in the Reichstag.

Although voters had clearly rejected Hitler and the Right, the election

Old-guard government dignitaries attend a performance at Berlin's State Opera House during the hopeful year 1928. Second from left is Foreign Minister Gustav Stresemann. In the middle, wearing medals, sits portly President Hindenburg.

otherwise left the German political picture in a muddle. Socialists and Communists increased their share of the vote, although their total was well short of a majority, while the center-to-right parties that had been running the coalition government lost support. President Hindenburg had patched together one short-term coalition after another, but the continued fragmentation of the Reichstag could eventually paralyze the republic. If that occurred, Hitler and his Nazis might loom as an attractive alternative.

Despite its political floundering, the German nation was regaining international stature and economic strength—conditions that fostered the well-being of the citizenry and thereby diminished the prospects of the Nazis, who thrived on discontent. Foreign Minister Gustav Stresemann had engineered a dazzling succession of diplomatic coups: evacuation of the Ruhr by occupying troops, the Locarno Pact, German entry into the League of Nations, and the Treaty of Berlin, which reaffirmed earlier bonds with Soviet Russia. In 1928, he topped the list by adding his signature to the Kellogg-Briand Pact, in which fifteen nations renounced war. Despite the agitation of the Nazis and Nationalists who decried Germany's tattered pride, the fatherland was once again an acknowledged great power. For his adroit diplomacy, Stresemann shared a Nobel Peace Prize with France's respected foreign minister, Aristide Briand.

For the most part, the economic vista in 1928 seemed sunny. Social ills did fester in parts of the society. Foreign loans to German industries had spawned automation in factories, which cost some workers their jobs. Agricultural income was declining, and a number of farmers, unable to pay their bank debts, were losing their farms. But other signs were cheering. Fueled by the loans from abroad, production was increasing faster than elsewhere in Europe and had already surpassed Germany's prewar levels. The standard of living in general was rising, sales and wages were up, social measures such as unemployment insurance and an eight-hour day were on the books, and handsome buildings were sprouting all over Germany.

Some journalists declared nazism dead in the wake of the 1928 elections, just as others had lowered the curtain on the movement when Hitler was jailed in 1923. Indeed, the Führer's name appeared only rarely on front pages, and a history of the Weimar regime completed in mid-1929 declared that the republic's foes had "receded into the background."

But Hitler, who seemed oddly content, was in fact biding his time, ready to strike when the moment was right. Nazism was still on the outer fringe of German politics, to be sure, and Hitler was little known outside Bavaria, but he had built a tight-knit, well-disciplined, and fiercely loyal revolutionary band that was enthralled by its leader's fanaticism. If he could sustain the party's momentum, nazism might evolve into a mass movement that he could manipulate with his consummate demagogic skills. All he lacked was a spark, something to ignite the tinder of German rage and nationalistic fervor—and he would soon get it.

Goebbels had offered a forthright preview of Nazi tactics just before the 1928 elections: "We will become Reichstag deputies in order to cripple the Weimar mentality with its own type of machinery," he wrote. "We come as enemies. We come like the wolf that breaks into the sheepfold!"

Seventy leaders of the Nazi party descended on Munich in early September of 1928 to hear Hitler appraise how far they had come and how far they had yet to go. He was pleased to report that the "Führer principle" —his personal totalitarian rule of the party—had been firmly established. He also noted that Nazi-inspired antipathy toward the Jews was on the increase. "What was hardly there ten years ago," he said, "is there today." Confident as always, Hitler assured his disciples of ultimate victory. Their task, he said, was to educate Germans in "fanatical nationalism" and lead them away from "the delirium of democracy." Hitler then condensed into a few harsh lines the savage and cynical world-view that had brought him this far: "As we deliver the people from the atmosphere of pitiable belief in possibilities that lie outside the bounds of one's own strength—such as the belief in reconciliation, understanding, world peace, the League of Nations, and international solidarity—we destroy those ideas. There is only one right in the world, and that right is one's own strength." ✠

A Republic Beset by Hard Times

Hitler's drive to power received an incalculable boost from the economic trials that left Germany ripe for radical change. One such ordeal—the inflation sparked by Germany's huge war debt—reached its peak in November of 1923. As officials tried to meet federal obligations by printing money around the clock, the mark tumbled precipitately in value until more than four trillion were needed to fetch a single American dollar. "The inflation put an end to my endeavors," recalled one small-business owner. "Hunger and privation once more held sway in my home. I cursed the government that sanctioned such misery." Like many others, the frustrated entrepreneur heeded Hitler's defiant words and joined the Nazi party.

In 1924, the economic turmoil subsided as domestic austerity and foreign loans stabilized the mark. But the American stock-market crash five years later brought Germans new distress. Banks that had handed out inflated currency by the bagful in 1923 now locked their doors. Middle-class citizens who had weathered the first storm by pawning their prize possessions now begged in the streets for work. There were too many hungry and homeless for Germany's welfare system to cope with, and thousands of the destitute resorted to scavenging or stealing. Others turned to prostitution and drug running or joined one of the extremist parties that promised simplistic answers and a hot meal.

No group was more successful than the Nazis at capitalizing on this era of ill feelings. In the words of Joseph Goebbels, Hitler's party was ever ready "to organize hatred and despair with ice-cold calculation."

An unemployed man stands on a Cologne corner in 1928. In a year, more than a million Germans would need work.

A housewife uses nearly worthless marks as kindling for her stove during the inflation of 1923. Hitler labeled the printing of these "scraps of paper" a criminal act. "The state itself," he said, "has become the biggest swindler and crook."

Depositors mill about the closed doors of the Berliner Stadtbank after the collapse of major German banks in 1931.

A bank's shattered windows testify to the anger of Berliners who took to the streets in 1931 to decry economic conditions. Nazi deputies in the Reichstag exploited the discontent by demanding that the holdings of all "bank and stock-exchange magnates" be expropriated.

A stolid victim of the Great Depression advertises his readiness to accept "work of any kind." By the time Hitler launched his 1932 presidential campaign, six million Germans were registered as unemployed.

Ich suche Arbeit jeder Art!

The jobless queue up outside an employment office in Hanover in 1932 near a wall bearing the words "Elect Hitler!"

Well-dressed Germans part with household treasures to avoid ruin during the inflation of 1923. The economic crisis wiped out the savings of many middle-class families, who then became targets for the politics of alienation advanced by the Nazis.

A German mother and her child pick currants from the debris lining the gutter of an outdoor market in the year 1930. Hunger came to be so acute during the depression that armed farmers—who faced privation themselves on account of falling prices—stood guard in their fields by night to fend off foragers.

Berliners eat a free meal during yuletide in 1923. A youth whose father lost his job was quick to fix blame: "Hatred flared up in me against the regime."

Displaced by the depression, squatters in the coal district of Silesia peer from the dank recesses of their shelter.

A drug dealer *(left)* slips cocaine into the lining of a hat. Drug traffic and rampant prostitution led Hitler to vow to combat the "moral plague" that infected Germany's cities.

A young woman attracts admirers in Hamburg's red-light district in 1929.

Underworld figures congregate at a dimly lit bar in Berlin. Police closed this hangout after the Nazis came to power.

Berlin patrolmen pursue protesters during the 1929 May Day rally. The police shot thirty-one Communists.

An unidentified radical tangles with police in Berlin. Such conflict, fueled by rising unemployment, persisted in the streets until the new Nazi regime turned loose the police in a brutal crackdown on dissidents.

The Arts in a Nation on Edge

Top: Bauhaus signet designed by Oskar Schlemmer, 1922

The Germany that emerged from the ordeal of the Great War was a society askew. To many citizens, the political and economic dislocations of the postwar era were deeply unsettling. But to Germany's artistic avant-garde, the sense of living in a culture cut loose from its moorings was exhilarating. "A world has come to an end," exulted Walter Gropius, founder of the experimental school of design known as the Bauhaus. "We must seek a radical solution to our problems."

For some artists, the search was overtly political. Caricaturist George Grosz joined the Communist party and produced scathing portraits of ruling-class decadence (page 51). Leftist lyricist and playwright Bertolt Brecht chose a more seductive approach, using Berlin's racy cabaret tradition to enliven his somber visions of social conflict. German filmmakers, meanwhile, tended to avoid polemics; they proclaimed their independence by creating mesmerizing studies of murderers and other misfits.

What the leading talents of this turbulent age had in common was a refusal to be bound by the conventions of the past. Painter Felix Nussbaum summed up that spirit in a 1931 work shown here, in which progressive artists stage an impromptu exhibit at Berlin's Brandenburg Gate while disdainful members of the Academy of Fine Arts pass in mourning.

The resistance that rebels such as Nussbaum encountered from the Weimar establishment was benign when compared with the treatment that awaited them from the Nazis, who marked their rise to power by destroying books and paintings they considered provocative. Nussbaum himself, facing persecution as both a Jew and an exponent of the attitude the Nazis branded "culture bolshevism," was one of many hundred artists who fled the regime in the 1930s. Some found safe haven; others shared the fate of Nussbaum, who was arrested by the Gestapo in Belgium after a decade in exile and died at Auschwitz.

"There is still a lot of muck to be carted away," wrote George Grosz in 1925, "and I am happy to take part in this work." For Grosz and his fellow artistic muckraker, Otto Dix, a painter's mission was to expose society's contradictions—an effect they achieved by juxtaposing portraits of vagrants or war victims with images of the rich at play.

Other German artists of the era defined their role more idealistically. Members of the November Group, inspired by the overthrow of the imperial order in November 1918, dedicated themselves to the "moral regeneration of a young and free Germany"—a credo that did not prevent critics from denouncing their unorthodox works as degenerate. Traditionalists had an equally hard time accepting the style fostered by Gropius and his colleagues at the Bauhaus in Weimar. Inspired by mentors such as Wassily Kandinsky, students there renounced fusty German conventions and created useful objects that followed the austere lines of abstract paintings. A cherished principle of the Bauhaus was that artists must embrace new technologies—an idea exemplified in Erich Salomon's photography. He used the small, hand-held camera invented in Germany to catch his subjects unawares, bringing a fresh spontaneity to his craft.

Adopting a Radical Perspective

Photographer Erich Salomon

Einstein Tower, by Erich Mendelsohn of the November Group, 1920

November Group artists preparing for a 1924 exhibit

Wassily Kandinsky's *On White*, 1923

Painter Otto Dix

The Waltz, by George Grosz, 1921

Poster for a Bauhaus exhibit, 1923

A Soaring Season for Song and Dance

For performing artists, the twenties were indeed golden. Through good times and bad, Berlin sustained a vibrant nightlife that other cities tried to emulate. In the streets and onstage, anything was possible. The spirit was summed up in the cabarets, where masters of ceremonies poked fun at the powerful between wicked stage acts that could be as daring as anything German artists put on canvas. The dancer Anita Berber performed without a costume and, it was said, met catcalls "with an obscene gesture." Serious performers and composers provoked audiences in subtler ways. The choreographer Oskar Schlemmer and dancer Harald Kreutzberg contorted the movements of ballet. Paul Hindemith rejected that German music should be rooted in German traditions and wove jazz motifs into his scores. And Max Brand jarred operagoers with his work *Maschinist Hopkins,* set in a factory. But the stage sensation was Brecht's *Threepenny Opera.* Graced by the efforts of composer Kurt Weill and his wife, singer Lotte Lenya, the musical celebrated its lowlife characters as forthright villains in a world of hypocrites.

A Schlemmer ballet clown, 1927

Maschinist Hopkins, 1929

A score by Hindemith, c.1925

Lotte Lenya and Kurt Weill

A Threepenny Opera ad, 1928

Berlin cabaret performers

Harald Kreutzberg

Bertolt Brecht

Cover for Döblin's *Berlin Alexanderplatz*, 1929

Scene from a play by Franz Werfel, 1921

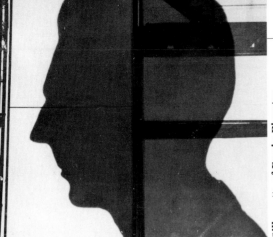

Silhouette of Erwin Piscator

Thomas Mann accepting the Nobel Prize, 1929

An Angry Legacy of Dissent

"We must sweep away with an iron broom all that is rotten in Germany," political commentator Kurt Tucholsky wrote after the First World War, a conflict in which he and many other angry young writers learned to despise the old order and its flag-waving apologists. "We will get nowhere if we wrap our heads in a black, white, and red rag and whisper anxiously, 'Later, my good fellow, later.'"

For playwright and producer Erwin Piscator, who staged his first efforts for his fellow soldiers at the front, the war was symptomatic of social ills that could be cured only through a Marxist revolution. In 1919, he founded the Proletarian Theater in a working-class district of Berlin. His experimental productions there enjoyed little popular success, but he influenced such rising talents as Bertolt Brecht and Erich Mühsam, who wrote a play defending the American anarchists Sacco and Vanzetti and later died in a Nazi concentration camp.

Even those writers whose concerns were more personal than political cast a critical eye on society. Franz Werfel—author of poems, plays, and novels—dramatized the bitterness between sons and fathers in an authoritarian culture. The physician and novelist Alfred Döblin deftly probed urban decay in his epic, *Berlin Alexanderplatz*. And Thomas Mann set his masterwork *The Magic Mountain* in a sanatorium on the eve of the Great War to examine the romantic German compulsion to cast off reason and restraint and court death.

Erich Mühsam (*center*) with two literary comrades

Peter Lorre in a scene from *M*, 1931

Poster for *Metropolis*, 1927

Poster for *The Cabinet of Dr. Caligari*, 1919

German cinema during the Weimar era mirrored the anxieties of the culture. To be sure, there were fine directors such as Ernst Lubitsch who soothed moviegoers by evoking times past or the glories of nature. But some of the best films of the day sounded a chillingly prophetic note, portraying a world dominated by irrational forces.

This gloomy cinematic trend began in 1919 with the macabre Cabinet of Dr. Caligari. Shot against painted expressionist backdrops evoking the twisted visions of the insane, the film told of a circus somnambulist driven to murder by his keeper, the conjurer Caligari. Other mad manipulators darkened German screens in the years to come, but the sense of ungovernable impulses in the land was evoked more artfully in realistic films. In *The Blue Angel*, Marlene Dietrich won fame as a sultry cabaret artist who degrades her lover, a once-dignified professor, to helplessness. And in Fritz Lang's *M*, Peter Lorre played a child-killer at the mercy of his mania: "Always, there is this evil force inside me. I want to escape, but it's impossible. I have to obey it."

Lorre's grim words could have served as a motto for many of Hitler's followers. Yet ironically, the Führer was a fan of director Lang, having been charmed by his futuristic tale *Metropolis*, which depicted a world where rebellious workers and their masters are finally reconciled. Soon after the Nazi takeover, Joseph Goebbels visited Lang and offered him a government post. Calculating that escape was still possible, Lang asked for time to ponder the offer, and he fled to the city of Paris that night.

A top-hatted Marlene Dietrich in *The Blue Angel*, 1929

Ernst Lubitsch (seated) in the Alps

A vision of technology abused, from *Metropolis*

The fiery cultural counterrevolution that swept Nazi Germany in 1933 was years in the making. In the mid-twenties, Hitler made clear his contempt for modern art in *Mein Kampf*, branding the "bolshevized" works the "morbid excrescences of insane and degenerate men." Modernism was a scourge, like syphilis, Hitler argued, and the public must be protected from its carriers.

Hitler's ideas were buttressed in 1927 with the founding of the Nazi Fighting League for German Culture, dedicated to the suppression of artworks that smacked of foreign contagion—be it communism, cubism, or the "primitivism" of jazz. Such strictures were first systematically enforced in 1930, when Nazis joined a right-wing coalition government in Thuringia that banned progressive books and films and dismissed avant-garde artists from public posts. Three years later, Hitler's regime launched a more sweeping purge nationwide. Bonfires of books by purported radicals, including Nobel laureate Thomas Mann, flared in public squares and university courtyards. Many modern paintings burned as well, while others were pilloried in aesthetic horror shows that were presented to the public under slanted titles such as "The Spirit of November: Art in the Service of Sedition."

The Nazi crackdown effectively stifled artistic liberty in the Reich. But the extraordinary talents who were driven into exile carried the ferment of democratic Germany to new lands, where they offered up fresh challenges for free minds.

The burning of books in Berlin, May 10, 1933

TWO

An Uneasy
Coalition
of Conservatives

An intimidating image of nazism is projected in this poster featuring a hard-eyed Storm Trooper and the slogan "SA in the vanguard." By the early 1930s, the Nazis' brown-shirted army had become a menace to anyone who opposed the party— and was a threat even to Hitler.

ustav Stresemann, foreign minister of the Weimar Republic, was just fifty-one years old, but as he rose to speak to delegates representing the nations of the world at Geneva, he moved like an old man. His face was haggard, his eyes were sunken, and his suit hung in loose folds over his once-beefy frame. He had never been a stirring orator. His nasal delivery was marred by fits of coughing and a continuing struggle to find breath, symptoms of the exhaustion and heart ailment that afflicted him. On this day—September 9, 1929—he had less than a month left to live. Perhaps sensing the approaching end, he felt an urgent need to explain why the settlement he had recently concluded was in the best interests of his country, as well as those of Germany's former enemies.

After a year of intense negotiation, Stresemann had won a significant easing of the burdens placed on Germany by the Treaty of Versailles. The new pact had been hammered out in Paris at meetings chaired by an American banker, Owen D. Young; all sides had agreed to it in principle at a conference at the Hague in August. The accord limited for the first time the reparations Germany was to pay its former adversaries—a total of 121 billion marks in fifty-nine annual payments. As staggering as the financial terms were, they represented an improvement over the former plan, which had called for open-ended payments that were liable to grow as Germany's ability to pay increased. Stresemann had known that if he were to have any chance of selling the so-called Young Plan to his coalition-controlled government at home, he had to squeeze out additional benefits. Doggedly, he had wrested from the creditor nations relief from a number of controls that they had exerted over the German economy. More important, he had extracted from the obstinate French a promise that the last Allied soldiers would withdraw from the Rhineland by June 30, 1930, four and a half years earlier than the Versailles treaty had stipulated. Linking the economic and the political issues had been the keystone of Stresemann's negotiating plan. He had achieved success only through a last-minute personal appeal to his French counterpart, Aristide Briand, with whom he had shared the 1926 Nobel Peace Prize for improving Franco-German relations.

Stresemann barely gained international acceptance of the Young Plan. Increasingly ill, he had persevered with the greatest of effort and personal sacrifice. After one meeting at the Hague, he had utterly collapsed, crying, "I can go no further." Yet he had pulled himself together and won. The Young Plan, he hoped, would be the beginning of a reconciliation among former enemies, one that might eventually lead to a united Europe. "We have the modest task of bringing peoples closer to one another, of bridging differences," he told the delegates in Geneva. "Bear in mind," he added, "that the war of the future, even if one leaves out everything else, will have little place for personal heroism."

His work finished, the weary Stresemann stumbled home to Berlin for the last time. He died of a stroke on October 3, 1929, before the Young Plan won final approval in the Reichstag and, mercifully, before Stresemann or anyone else came to realize that the agreement he thought had earned a breathing space for his beleaguered republic had, in fact, united all its domestic enemies. One of them, an obscure extremist named Adolf Hitler, would seize upon the Young Plan and use it to transform himself into a figure of national stature.

In 1929, Hitler was the leader of a Bavarian-based splinter party that had become known chiefly for fighting in the streets. It was racked by internal fighting as well—among its pugnacious leaders, between its political functionaries and the paramilitary brawlers of the SA, between its nationalist and socialist wings. The party lacked connections or credibility with any other group or institution in Germany.

But it did not lack resourcefulness at the top. With the issue handed him by Stresemann, Hitler would begin two years of nonstop politicking that would carry him to the threshold of supreme power. He would stamp out the brushfires of dissent within his party and muzzle the ferocious SA. Then he would create partnerships with groups that had little in common with him or the Nazis. He would tap the purses of business people, outmaneuver the Weimar politicians, and harness for his own purposes an army that had long prided itself as the guardian of the German state.

German opposition to the Young Plan had begun to form even before the conference at the Hague. For all that it gained in limiting reparations, the

Exhausted French and German delegates, still wearing formal dinner attire, struggle to stay awake during an all-night negotiating session at the Hague, slowed by wrangling over petty details of the Young Plan.

◁ Foreign Minister Stresemann, who represented the Weimar Republic in negotiations over the Young Plan, believed that his nation should make economic sacrifices to gain political concessions from the Allies. "It is the duty of the German government," he argued, "to accept all bearable costs in order to win German freedom."

agreement still called for onerous payments to be made every year until 1988. Worse, it reaffirmed the clause of the hated Versailles treaty that had branded Germany with criminal guilt for starting World War I. Resentment of the treaty had been simmering for a decade, and the newly defined financial burden only made the treaty more galling.

A campaign to reject the Young Plan had been organized in July under the leadership of the head of the German Nationalist party, Alfred Hugenberg, a rotund sixty-three-year-old conservative. Hugenberg's aim was nothing less than to overthrow the republic and tear up the Versailles treaty. Ambitious and unscrupulous, he had amassed a personal fortune by combining politics with a variety of business ventures. For nine years, he had been chairman of the board of the giant Krupp munitions firm. By buying up newspaper companies, a large film studio, and a publishing house, Hugenberg had established a powerful pulpit in the German communications industry.

Characterizing the new reparations agreement as a "death penalty on the unborn" and the "Golgotha of the German people," Hugenberg formed a coalition of right-wing factions to end all reparations. His allies included the Stahlhelm, or Steel Helmets, a veterans' organization dear to the heart of President Hindenburg; the anti-Semitic, expansionist Pan-German League; and, significantly, two of Germany's disenchanted delegates to the Young committee—the general director of the United Steel Works, Albert

Vögler, and the president of the Reichsbank, Hjalmar Schacht, who represented powerful business and financial interests. The Nationalists planned to use the formidable sums of money and propaganda tools at their disposal to force passage of a so-called Law against the Enslavement of the German People. The act would not only renounce all foreign obligations, but call for the criminal prosecution of any government official who signed an agreement like the one Stresemann had negotiated.

Hugenberg and most of his supporters were also monarchists, intent on restoring the old imperial throne and the dominance of the aristocracy. Although the Nationalists had plenty of money, they now needed votes, and their appeal to ordinary folk was minuscule. To solve this problem, Hugenberg made what was to become a common mistake among right-wing German leaders; he decided he could use Hitler. Hugenberg met with Hitler in a Berlin club to enlist his help in the campaign for the plebiscite to renounce reparations.

Hitler at once recognized an unparalleled opportunity, and he moved quickly to exploit it. During the preceding three years, the German economy had enjoyed modest growth: Retail sales and wages were up, and unemployment stood at a manageable 650,000. Although the Nazi message of hate had gained few new adherents under such conditions, Hitler saw that the Young Plan could inflame the country. He was being offered the funding he needed to conduct his first national campaign in partnership with Germany's respectable, well-to-do conservatives, who until now had dismissed him as a disreputable fanatic.

Hitler's biggest problem, aside from lack of money, was the divisiveness within his own party. By January of 1929, he had completed a reorganization that reflected a fundamental change of direction—away from street-fighting aimed at revolution and toward electioneering designed to win power through the ballot box. He had changed the party from a paramilitary to a permanent campaign organization whose districts, or gaus, corresponded to the electoral districts. The centers of attention for the gaus were rural communities. Even in the disastrous 1928 elections, the Nazis had done relatively well there. Stresemann's success in maneuvering the nation back into the world community had hurt German agriculture. The stabilization of the mark had brought in a flood of foodstuffs from abroad, knocking the bottom out of domestic agricultural prices and causing a rash of farm foreclosures. Hitler's changes had increased the status of the Nazi political apparatus and diminished the power of the SA, which continued to function under the outmoded assumption that it would lead the violent overthrow of the government.

There was a second schism, this one within the political organization

Bis in die dritte Generation

Wehrt Euch!   Geht zum Volksbegehren!

müßt ihr fronen!

Under a driver's whip and the words "You must slave into the third generation!" workers labor at a grinding wheel in this placard urging voters to reject the Young Plan, which the Nazis assailed as a continuation of Germany's economic bondage.

itself. Hitler firmly controlled the southern, Bavarian wing of the party, based in Munich. But Gregor and Otto Strasser, in Berlin, retained a degree of power and independence that rankled Hitler. Gregor was the party's deputy führer and chief of organization, while Otto published an influential party newspaper. This was especially dangerous because the Strassers' beliefs about National Socialism differed markedly from Hitler's; they focused on the traditional tenets of socialism and championed the cause of the worker. This Socialist tilt was one reason why the party had received little funding from the industrialists. And the Strasser faction, for its part, would resist any alliance with the moneyed aristocracy.

Once Hitler was ready, he moved with such speed that neither the Strassers nor the SA had time to object. He agreed to join hands with Hugenberg, use his communications empire, and take the Nationalists' money but insisted that he have complete independence in formulating and disseminating propaganda. Hugenberg had sought a hireling, but in agreeing to Hitler's terms he created a full partner. Next, Hitler named Gregor Strasser to the joint finance committee, a position attractive enough to overcome any distaste Strasser felt about the alliance.

Everything about the new union must have seemed fortuitous to Hitler. Just as it was accomplished—at the same time the conference at the Hague was finishing work on the Young Plan—the Nazis held a party congress at Nuremberg, their first since 1927. That one had been a simple affair. This would be different. For months, Hitler had been urging his political organization to raise more funds and plan a dramatic spectacle. As a result, the 1929 event was the most lavishly mounted, best-attended, and most strident gathering yet. It featured bombastic speeches by the party's best orators, climaxing with a stemwinder by the Führer himself; a march-past by 60,000 uniformed troopers; enormous choreographed pageants showcased by theatrical lighting; an extravagant display of fireworks watched by a crowd of 150,000 people; and an emotional memorial ceremony honoring Germans killed in World War I. One of the honored guests was the retired German coal-industry magnate Emil Kirdorff, soon to become the first major industrialist to support the Nazi party. Hitler's opportunism was already bringing results.

The campaign to pass the Law against the Enslavement of the German People had three phases. The first, an initiative to introduce the legislation in the Reichstag, required that 10 percent of the country's voters approve it. In balloting held on October 16, after a month of frenzied campaigning, proponents of the law garnered four million votes, or 10.02 percent of those registered. This approximated the total vote the Nationalists had received in the 1928 elections and was a substantial improvement on the 810,000 votes the Nazis had won their last time out. The first hurdle had been cleared. But the Nazis still lacked influence in the Reichstag, and the Nationalists were not much better off. Together, the two parties held 85 seats in the 491-seat legislature. At that, they were able to deliver only 82 ayes when the legislation came to a vote.

Defeat in the Reichstag made necessary the third phase, bringing the issue before the public in a plebiscite. If a majority of Germany's 40 million voters approved the proposal, it would become law. But the balloting, held on December 22, was an embarrassing failure for the Nazi and the Nationalist parties; only 14 percent of the voters agreed with them. The Law against the Enslavement of the German People was a dead issue. Hitler, turning on Hugenberg, immediately heaped scorn on his erstwhile ally. He blamed the Nationalists' bourgeois inhibitions for the failure to enlist the support of the masses. But he was careful not to end his new relationship with Germany's business leaders.

By quickly abandoning Hugenberg, Hitler avoided the taint of failure, and cataclysmic economic events would soon provide him with an even more powerful issue. The depression was worsening; the American stock market had crashed in October, and banks in the United States had begun calling in their loans to German institutions. Refinancing was unavailable, and international trade was collapsing. The worse the situation became, the better the Nazis' invective sounded, and thanks to Hugenberg's newspapers, Hitler had become a household name to millions of Germans who had never heard of him before. The party coffers overflowed with money from dues, new memberships, and contributions from small-business owners who were beginning to see Hitler as a better bet than Hugenberg.

Even though the plebiscite failed, the Nazis did well in local voting. They elected a mayor in Coburg, Bavaria, and forced the appointment of their first provincial cabinet member; Wilhelm Frick was named interior minister of Thuringia. While working for the Munich police department—and eventually heading both its political and criminal sections—Frick had been an avid Nazi. He had participated in the Beer Hall Putsch and spied on his fellow officers for the party. Personally, Frick was a colorless man, but by virtue of his ministerial rank he became one of the most influential Nazis.

As 1930 began, the national economy continued to sputter, and the Nazi party flourished. It now counted more than 100,000 members, up about 30 percent from 1928. The new members were not destitute, but most feared that economic disaster might befall them in the near future. They willingly

Storm Troopers from the Rhineland stream through the medieval streets of Nuremberg to attend the 1929 Nazi party congress. The rally's purpose, said Hitler, was to show off nazism as "the young popular movement that must one day destroy that which is bringing destruction to Germany."

absorbed an increase in party dues and an assessment for the purchase of a new party headquarters.

With cash pouring in, Hitler moved the party into the elegant Barlow Palace, a spacious mansion overlooking the Königsplatz in Munich. He renamed the building Brown House and enthusiastically set about furnishing his office and a so-called Senate Hall with red leather chairs embossed with the Nazi eagle. He hung a portrait of himself (with the caption, "Nothing happens in this movement except what I wish!") and a painting of Frederick the Great and installed busts of such personal heroes as Otto von Bismarck and Italy's Benito Mussolini. Having created this lavish setting, he seldom used it, preferring instead to hold court among his admirers in the basement canteen. At the same time, he moved into an opulent nine-room apartment on another fashionable Munich street.

But the gloss provided by sudden affluence and minor electoral success did nothing to ease the political strains within the party. In fact, as Hitler's prominence increased, so did the threat of internal dissension. He led a party of the disaffected but was reaching out to the middle class and knitting a closer relationship with the wealthy elite. He commanded an army of thugs who expected to pommel the republic, but he knew that if his street fighters went too far, the army and the police could wipe them out, and he was determined to avoid another abortive putsch. In the face

of such irreconcilable differences, Hitler somehow managed to stay on the offensive.

In the spring of 1930, his tirades continued to arouse public feeling, but in the absence of an election and an effective opposition in the Reichstag, his lone voice did not hamper the Weimar government. So Hitler sent the Storm Troopers back into the streets to do battle with communists, Jews, and rival political parties. His purpose was to use violence and the threat of revolution to demoralize and even paralyze the government.

The struggle was really

Holding court in the basement canteen of Brown House, Hitler enthralls a group of Brownshirts. Maintaining the loyalty of these rebellious SA men while pursuing power through legal means required all of Hitler's manipulative skill.

Brown House, the Nazi party's imposing headquarters at 45 Briennerstrasse in Munich, was purchased with contributions from Rhineland industrialists and renovated under Hitler's supervision for its grand opening in January of 1931.

one of propaganda, however. Except when actually protecting a Nazi meeting or attacking an opposition gathering, the Brownshirts fought for neither territory nor tactical advantage but for show. The point of continually starting fights was to be seen fighting. As the current commander of the SA, Captain Franz Pfeffer von Salomon, put it, "If whole groups of people in planned fashion risk body, soul, and livelihood for a cause, it simply *must* be great and true."

Given the frustrations and uncertainties of life in Germany, it was easy enough to recruit roughnecks eager to bash heads. The difficulty was in keeping them from starting a civil war. The Storm Troopers saw themselves as soldiers who would win the eventual victory for the Nazi party. They expected to defeat and then become the army of Germany itself. Few understood yet that Hitler had no intention of permitting such a confrontation, that he intended to use the muscle of the SA where it was needed

Decorating the Brown Battalions

In 1924, an SA leader traveling in Austria notified party headquarters that he had found a stock of surplus Imperial German Army tropical shirts left over from World War I. Although Hitler disliked the shirts' brown color, the price was right, and the party purchased the entire lot as temporary uniforms for its Storm Troopers. The brown shirt endured and became the Nazis' trademark, worn until it was replaced by a tunic in the early 1930s.

As the SA grew in membership, insignia for its uniforms proliferated. Collar tabs *(opposite)* identified a wearer's district, unit, and rank. Imitating the regular army, many SA units adopted specialties, such as light infantry, aviation, and mountaineering, that were also identified on their collars. Decorations that originally signified participation in key party events were later awarded as badges of merit.

SA leaders were well aware of a uniform's intrinsic worth. A 1926 regulation stated that "a large number of uniformed and disciplined men, marching in step, will impress every German deeply and speak to his heart in a more convincing and moving way than any written or spoken logic ever can."

A *Scharführer*, or staff sergeant, of the 88th Regiment based in Hessen wore the shirt and kepi above. The 1932 service tunic at right, above, belonged to an engineer-sergeant in Berlin.

The color of a collar device indicated the wearer's gau, or district. Pips denoted junior ranks; oak leaves, senior.

Tabs worn on the right collar signified an SA man's *Standarte* (regiment), *Sturm* (company), and his unit's specialty.

The collar tabs shown above indicate cavalry *(left)*, aviation *(center)*, and infantry—the 28th Company, 158th Regiment.

This badge was awarded in 1933 to men who had marched in the 1923 Munich putsch.

The Braunschweig badge became an official award in 1936.

Participants in the 1929 Nuremberg rally received this badge.

The badge commemorating the October 1922 rally in Coburg was one of the party's highest decorations.

to instill fear and confusion, then dismantle it. In the spring of 1930, however, fear and confusion were Hitler's stock in trade, and he loosened the reins of the Storm Troopers, leaving for later the question of how to bring its legion back under control.

Street violence spread across the country, swirling through cities and villages like dust devils preceding a storm. Nazi propagandist Joseph Goebbels applied his formidable skills to whipping up the frenzy of the street brawlers. One of his virtuoso performances was inspired by the death of twenty-two-year-old Horst Wessel, a preacher's son and apostate who had been living with a former prostitute in a Berlin slum. The young man, a Nazi, was shot by a rival for his mistress's affections. The gunman happened to be a communist. Goebbels transformed the squalid killing into a political assassination and the dead youth into a Nazi martyr. A propagandistic paean to the SA that Wessel had written was elevated into the party hymn—"The Horst Wessel Song" *(pages 74-75).*

The SA was doing exactly what Hitler wanted done—demonstrating the powerlessness of the Weimar government and the power of the Nazis. But at every turn, things threatened to get out of hand. The increasingly worried government began to crack down. In June of 1930, Bavaria and Prussia outlawed the wearing of the brown shirt, and SA members responded by wearing white shirts, or none at all. Prussia went further, forbidding state employees to join either the Nazi or the Communist party.

Then, as the SA became ever more unruly and the government more threatening, the Nazi party suddenly split along its other major fissure—between the socialist Strasser wing and the nationalist Hitler wing. By this time, Gregor Strasser had been summoned to Munich to become the party's chief political organizer, but his brother Otto had remained in Berlin, where he was publishing several newspapers, including the official Nazi journal for northern Germany. In April of 1930, all of Otto Strasser's newspapers trumpeted support for the trade unions of Saxony, which had declared a general strike.

Hitler had to act. If he threw his support behind Otto Strasser, he might alienate the conservative business element he was so anxious to woo. But failure to support Strasser risked a major party rift. For a month, he temporized, looking for an easy out. Finding none, he went to Berlin on May 21 and confronted Strasser in a contentious meeting that continued for two days. Hitler tried to win Strasser's submission with every technique at his command—debate of the issues, soulful appeals to party loyalty, promises of rewards, dire threats. But the Führer was up against a man as stubborn as himself; Strasser believed that Hitler was betraying the Nazi party's ideals. "I never make a mistake," Hitler bellowed at one point. "Every one of my words is historic!" Strasser remained unimpressed and recalcitrant.

Hitler returned to the southern city of Munich with the schism unresolved, and for yet another month he dithered. When at the end of June he took action, it was indirect. He ordered Goebbels to purge the party of all "rootless scribblers or unruly parlor Bolsheviks." Goebbels immediately understood what was meant and expelled Strasser. After a brief attempt to pursue his socialist objectives with a Nazi party of his own, Otto Strasser faded from public life.

Before the break with Strasser could be repaired or the continuing strains between the party and the SA soothed, circumstance handed the Nazis a victory by default: The Weimar Republic began its final disintegration.

In March of 1930, shortly after ratifying the Young Plan, the fractious Reichstag had once again refused to support Chancellor Hermann Müller. This time, the issue concerned unemployment compensation. Failing to find a solution, Müller resigned. His frustration was widely shared throughout the nation. Since the Weimar Republic's inception in the strife-torn days of a failing monarchy and a lost war, Germany had been plagued by an unstable party system. Müller's coalition government was the seventeenth in the republic's ten-year life span. There were so many parties, all fiercely unyielding on partisan matters, that taking even a minor action in the Reichstag involved lashing together a coalition that fell apart as soon as the next matter came before it. President Hindenburg and the army had maintained a decorous distance from politics, as the constitution required, but now the danger of governmental paralysis prompted a fateful change.

An important instrument of that change was an army officer named Kurt von Schleicher. The forty-eight-year-old major general had begun his career in 1900 as a subaltern in Hindenburg's regiment, the 3d Foot Guards, where he had made a lifelong friend of Oskar von Hindenburg, son of the future president. Schleicher had seen little action during the war but impressed many people with his quick mind, urbane manners, and gift for diplomacy. He could no more avoid politics, as a good army officer was supposed to do, than he could avoid breathing. In 1929, Schleicher's superior officer, General Wilhelm Groener, the minister of defense, gave his protégé the opportunity to become a behind-the-scenes player in German politics by making him responsible for liaison between the army and the civilian government.

Schleicher took to the work avidly. At first, he was content with advancing his friends and ruining his enemies in the army. For instance, he had General Werner von Blomberg removed as the army's second in command and replaced by General Kurt von Hammerstein. By 1930, Schleicher had begun to operate on a larger scale. He suggested that Hindenburg become involved in the politics of the Reichstag and select the next chancellor.

The idea was to replace the wrangling impotence of the Reichstag with the firm guidance of a strong chancellor who could rule effectively without the support of a stable parliamentary coalition. If differences between parties became irreconcilable and a majority vote unobtainable, the chancellor would appeal to the president to invoke article 48 of the Weimar constitution, a clause that allowed the president to suspend civil rights and to govern by emergency decree.

This scenario appealed to the aging Hindenburg, who was increasingly distressed by the inability of the politicians to forget their partisan stands and think of Germany first. And the man Schleicher proposed as chancellor was appealing to the army, too. He was Heinrich Brüning, leader of the Catholic Center party, a war hero, a man of unquestionable patriotism. Hoping to save his country, Hindenburg—urged by the calculating Schleicher—agreed to the plan. On March 27, 1930, Brüning became chancellor.

It was a monumental miscalculation. Three months after taking office, Brüning could not get a financial program through the Reichstag, so he followed the agreed-upon formula. He asked Hindenburg to approve the necessary legislation by emergency decree. But when Hindenburg complied, the Reichstag demanded that the decree be withdrawn. A less-scrupulous man might have ignored the request, but Brüning felt compelled to take the matter to the people. He dissolved the Reichstag and set new elections for September 14. Thus

Creating the Legend of Horst Wessel

In Berlin on January 14, 1930, a twenty-two-year-old neighborhood SA leader named Horst Wessel was surprised and mortally wounded in his apartment by a Communist gunman. Except that the man who pulled the trigger, one Albrecht Höhler, was also a jealous rival for the affections of Wessel's ex-prostitute girlfriend, the shooting differed little from the scores of other bloody Nazi-communist confrontations plaguing Germany's cities. The incident would have passed without notice but for a stirring patriotic song Wessel had written titled "Die Fahne hoch" (Raise high the flag). The lyrics, which were set to a rousing North Sea folk tune, glorified Nazi Storm Troopers who had given their lives for the cause. Three months before he was wounded, Wessel had submitted the song to the Nazi newspaper *Der Angriff*, where it caught the eye of the editor, Joseph Goebbels.

When Goebbels learned that the young lyricist lay dying in a hospital bed, he sensed a propaganda bonanza and set out to transform Wessel into a political martyr. Goebbels unabashedly described the street fighter as a "socialist Christ" who had forgone his university studies to devote his life to national socialism. On February 7, Goebbels arranged to have Wessel's song performed in public for the first time at a Nazi party rally in the Berlin Sportpalast. It became an instant sensation.

Sixteen days later, Wessel died of his wounds and Goebbels staged an elaborate funeral. The communists played into his hands by harassing the cortege and holding a counter-demonstration outside the cemetery. At graveside, Goebbels dramatically called the SA roll. When he reached Wessel's name, the rows of uniformed Storm Troopers shouted in unison, "Present!"

After it was renamed "The Horst Wessel Song," the piece went on to become the offical hymn of the Nazi party—and it was heard in Germany more frequently than any other music except "Deutschland Über Alles," the national anthem.

possessing a clear conscience, he sealed the fate of German democracy.

Once again, Hitler saw opportunity and moved to grasp it. In most respects, the timing of the elections could not have been more propitious for him. He had reorganized his party, rid himself of at least one of the Strassers, established fresh sources of revenue, and settled into opulent new headquarters. The economy was unraveling, frightening the public and making people more receptive than ever before to his railings against the Weimar "traitors" and the Jews. Successes in state and local elections had followed his round of intense national exposure in the campaign against the Young

Fists clenched in determination, Horst Wessel appears on the cover of the sheet music for his song just as the lyrics described his martyred SA comrades— still marching forward, in spirit, toward the day when "Hitler's banners shall wave unchecked."

Plan—the plebiscite's failure was now a minor footnote, ascribed to Hugenberg. In all, Hitler was confident that he could move the Nazis well forward in the pack of ten parties represented in the Reichstag. But as he took the first steps in the new election campaign, disaster struck.

In August of 1930, the Berlin contingent of the SA revolted in anger over funding. One Storm Trooper wrote in frustration to Gregor Strasser that he had been arrested more than thirty times and convicted eight times for "assault and battery, resistance to a police officer, and other such misdemeanors that are natural for a Nazi." In the course of this activity, he said, he had been wounded at least twenty times. "I have knife scars on the back of my head, on my left shoulder, on my lower lip, on my right cheek, on the left side of my upper lip, and on my right arm." For all this, he had not "claimed or received a penny of party money" and, having spent his inheritance, was "facing financial ruin."

Serious as such cases were, the underlying issue was power. All along, the SA had regarded itself as the instrument of the German revolution. The role of the politicians, in its view, was secondary to the muscle of determined men. Yet the SA found itself unrewarded by the Nazi party. Requests from the SA for representation in the Reichstag delegation, and for permission to increase training, fell on deaf ears. "As far as the political organization is concerned," a Brownshirt officer wrote, "the SA is here just to die."

The SA toughs had by long habit settled things with fists and truncheons, and they saw no reason to change when dealing with their own party. At the end of August, they stormed Nazi headquarters in Berlin and, after a pitched battle with Hitler's elite guard, the black-shirted SS, wrecked the building and its contents. To his intense embarrassment, district leader Goebbels had to call the civilian police to evict the rebels from the building.

Appalled, Hitler rushed to Berlin. Through a long night, he drove from beer hall to beer hall, joining the Storm Troopers at their tables to plead and weep, blaming the whole affair on misguided party officials who had come between him and his beloved Storm Troopers. He turned on the full force of his mesmerizing rhetoric, speaking of the great victories that were now imminent, recalling how far they had come together. But Hitler did not rely on oratory alone; he also

General Kurt von Schleicher, in civilian clothes, was Machiavellian after Defense Minister Groener made him an adviser in 1929. Groener called Schleicher "my cardinal in politics."

Chancellor Heinrich Brüning *(hand on chin)* meets with his cabinet in the chancellery garden in Berlin on a summer day in 1930. Brüning's policy of economic belt-tightening prompted the Nazis to deride him as the "hunger chancellor."

promised better funding. To accomplish this, he would level a special assessment on the entire party.

One after another, the groups of sullen men returned to the fold. A weary Hitler returned to Munich, waited a few days, then ordered the retirement of the SA commander, Pfeffer. Hitler appointed himself supreme leader of the SA. As a precaution against future mutinies, he required every SA member to swear an oath of unconditional loyalty to him.

With the breach thus patched over, Hitler returned to the election. His campaign was a propaganda masterpiece, a triumph of form over substance. Nazi organizers plastered every available wall with posters and slogans. They conducted countless band concerts, field days, and open meetings to woo the frustrated citizenry with the party line. Speakers from the 2,000 graduates of the Nazi orators' school addressed small assemblies; brighter party luminaries, such as Göring or Goebbels, graced major gatherings; and the Führer himself, who during the course of the campaign was in constant motion, crisscrossing Germany, spoke at an impressive number of large rallies (twenty in six weeks).

The Nazis offered no program for easing the effects of the depression and no details about how Germany would regain greatness. Hitler and his minions delivered only invective, accusing those they held responsible for the present state of affairs—the Jews, the corrupt politicians, the communists, the hypocritical Allied powers. This diatribe against the people in government, written by Goebbels, was typical: "Throw the scum out! Tear the masks off their mugs! Take them by the scruff of the neck and kick them in their fat bellies on September 14 and sweep them out of the temple with trumpets and drums!"

Nor was it only the words that were vicious. During 1930, nearly 60,000 political assemblies of various kinds were held in Prussia alone. Few of these meetings took place without violence, and in nine of ten cases, according to the police, the fighting was started by either the SA or its communist counterpart, the Red-Front Fighters' League. "Ordinary brawls had given way to murderous attacks," the chief of police in Berlin later wrote. "Knives, blackjacks, and revolvers had replaced political argument."

The Nazis' middle-class opponents regarded the rallies with disdain, one observer branding them a "stupid enthusiasm." The stiff-armed Nazi salute, the shouts of "Heil Hitler!" accompanied by clicking heels, and the reverent use of the title "der Führer," all of which saw widespread use for the first time in the late summer of 1930, struck outsiders as ridiculous. A satirist said of Hitler, "The man doesn't exist; he is only the noise he makes." But the Führer was confident he was getting through to the people and predicted a gain of 50 seats in the Reichstag.

The reality stunned Hitler as much as anyone. The Nazis received 6.4 million of the votes cast on September 14. With 107 Reichstag deputies, they were suddenly the second most powerful party in Germany. The Social Democrats, with 143 seats, still had the largest contingent in the legislature, but along with the other moderate parties their base seriously eroded. Only the Nazis and the Communists increased their strength. The possibility of forming a stable coalition government became even more remote.

Hitler had no intention of using his increased strength in the Reichstag to help govern the country. "We are a parliamentary party by compulsion," he declared in Munich ten days after the election. "This victory we have just won is nothing but a new weapon for our struggle." While his statement was calculated to hint at armed revolution, Hitler clung to legal means of increasing his power, and he withheld from President Hindenburg and the disciplined German army an excuse to move against him with force. As the Nazi leader recognized, only the army now had the power to stop him, and on the day following his Munich speech he moved boldly toward winning its support.

The officer corps was worried. It was well known that ex-soldiers in the SA wanted to take over the army. Nor was it a secret that the combined personnel of the SA and SS surpassed 100,000 men, exceeding the number of troops in the army. Officials were not reassured to uncover, early in 1930,

A pair of young Storm Troopers fasten a campaign poster for Hitler to a barn door. The Nazis wooed the farm vote by promising to halt agricultural imports and channel funds to farmers for soil improvement, better seed, and new machinery.

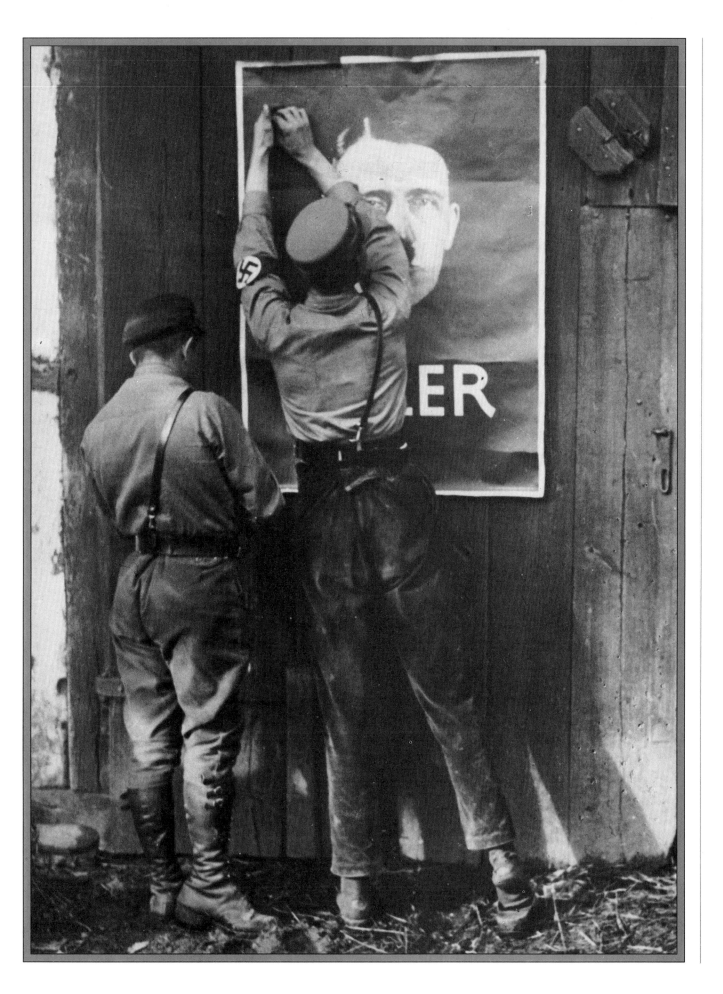

a campaign by three brash lieutenants to recruit their fellow officers into the Nazi party. On September 23, the lieutenants went on trial before the Supreme Court at Leipzig, and on September 25 the defense called Adolf Hitler to take the stand.

The lieutenants' fate did not concern Hitler. He had a message for the leaders of the army, and he knew his testimony would receive their closest attention. "None of us are interested in replacing the army," he purred. "My only wish is that the German state and the German people be imbued with a new spirit." He insisted that, in seeking this goal, he had ordered his subordinates to use only legal means and that he had expelled from the party those who did not. He cited as an example "Otto Strasser, who toyed with the idea of revolution."

He had done everything he could, Hitler protested, to prevent the Brown-shirts "from assuming any kind of military character." The German army need not worry about the Storm Troopers, he said, because their exclusive purpose was to protect the Nazi party, not to challenge the state. Then he added, telling the truth for a change, "I have been a soldier long enough to know that it is impossible for a party organization to fight against the disciplined forces of the army."

At the same time, however, Hitler had arranged for the return of former SA commander Ernst Röhm, who had been eased out earlier after heated arguments with the Führer over control of that organization. Shortly after Hitler had blandly assured the court of the nonmilitary nature of the SA, Röhm—serving as chief of staff because Hitler retained the title of supreme leader—would militarize the Storm Troopers even further, using traditional army methods of organization and discipline.

Nonetheless, after smoothing the feathers of the officer corps, Hitler threw a bone to his Storm Troopers. At the end of his discourse at the trial about legality and principle, he added an icy threat: "When the Nazi movement's struggle is successful, then there will be a Nazi Court of Justice, too. The November 1918 revolution will be avenged, and heads will roll." It was this ominous remark, and not the otherwise conciliatory address to the court, that was confirmed a fortnight later when the newly elected Nazis took their places in the Reichstag. Wearing brown shirts instead of business suits, they responded to the roll call by bellowing, "Present, Heil Hitler!" and shouted insults and epithets at the other deputies. Here, in the scornful words of Social Democratic deputy Toni Sender, were the self-proclaimed "elite of the 'Aryan' race—this noisy, shouting, uniformed gang." Sender wrote that, as she studied them, she became terrified by what she saw: "So many men with the faces of criminals and degenerates. What a degradation to sit in the same place with such a gang!"

Yet the army was reassured by Hitler's performance at the trial. (The lieutenants drew slap-on-the-wrist prison terms.) General Groener's political liaison, Kurt von Schleicher, responded with an overture to the Nazis. The election results had hamstrung the Brüning government. Although, through President Hindenburg, the army had great influence over the issuing of emergency decrees, this autocratic method could not be used for long in the absence of broad popular support. The army feared an armed uprising by either the Nazis or the Communists and dreaded a revolution by both parties at once.

Of the two radical parties, the National Socialists with their six million votes were obviously stronger and growing faster. Moreover, they were nationalistic. Schleicher was convinced that the Nazis represented the lesser of the two evils and that he could handle Hitler. He had the backing of General Groener, his anti-Nazi boss, who hoped to bind Hitler "doubly and triply to the stake of legality." Working as always behind the scenes, Schleicher communicated to Röhm and Gregor Strasser that he was interested in more contact with Hitler. In January of 1931, he sent a louder signal by allowing Nazis to enlist in the army and be employed by the army in sensitive civilian jobs.

Hitler was delighted by these developments but had to move carefully. Just as his alliance with the Nationalists had galled the socialists in his party, so any accommodation with the army would be anathema to the SA. Determined nevertheless to respond to Schleicher's overtures, Hitler in February reaffirmed his dedication to legal political processes and forbade any more street-fighting.

Immediately, the Brownshirts became restive. Hitler had only papered over their grievances the previous August; the Storm Troopers still burned with resentment as they saw the fruits of success going to the political functionaries, and their longed-for day of reckoning indefinitely postponed. Now they were being watched more closely. When a group of dissidents under the direction of a former police captain named Walter Stennes, the SA commander of eastern Germany, planned another mutiny, the SS warned the Führer before the malcontents could act. Hitler derailed the rebellion by sacking Stennes.

Meanwhile, Germany's economic plight worsened. The contraction of international trade forced factories to shut down. Either they could no longer afford raw materials or their products were too expensive for their customers. During the six months ending in March 1931, unemployment increased by more than 50 percent, to 4.75 million persons. Germany faced the danger of a massive banking collapse. The foreign banks whose loans had fueled recovery now demanded repayment, an impossible burden for a country already saddled with huge reparations payments. Fearing the loss of their lifetime savings, German depositors queued up to withdraw their money before it was too late. When one of Germany's largest banks, the Darmstädter und National, failed in July, following the collapse in May of Austria's biggest, the Kreditanstalt, the government was forced to close all banks temporarily.

The Brüning government strove to remain solvent by imposing austerity on a nation already in dire straits. Emergency decrees raised taxes, lowered wages, and reduced unemployment benefits. The new foreign minister tried to improve trade by negotiating an end to the customs barriers between Germany and Austria, but, as always, France was afraid that Germany would rebound too quickly. Claiming such an agreement would be a violation of the Treaty of Versailles, the French blocked the proposal in the World Court, humiliating Brüning. Deprivation and fear reached unbearable levels. There was a widespread feeling that something terrible was about to happen. When the ambassador from Great Britain returned to Berlin after a brief absence in mid-July, he was struck "by an atmosphere of extreme tension."

The Nazis, on the other hand, thought everything was going splendidly. As Gregor Strasser had declared two years earlier, "All that serves to precipitate the catastrophe is good, very good, for us and our German revolution." His belief was borne out by repeated successes at the polls. In the last eight provincial elections held in 1931, the Nazis received an average of 35 percent of the vote; the comparable figure in 1930 had been only 18 percent. Hitler was ecstatic: "Never in my life have I been so well disposed and inwardly contented as in these days, for hard reality has opened the eyes of millions of Germans." Yet in truth Hitler and the Nazis remained too weak to decisively influence events. The great majority of German voters still supported other parties and leaders. By itself, the Nazi delegation to the Reichstag, though a force to be reckoned with, could accomplish nothing.

Then, without warning, Hitler found himself confronted by a personal adversary he could not outmaneuver—death. He had been keeping com-

Each member of the Nazi party received an identification card such as this one, listing name, address, occupation, and birth date, and signed by a party leader. At the end of 1931, more than half a million Germans had become card-carrying Nazis.

The Bogus Threat of a Red Revolt

Among the Weimar Republic's welter of political parties, only the German Communist party (KPD) could match the Nazis in partisan zeal. But in the battle for the hearts and minds of the German masses, the Communists failed dismally.

The roots of the failure lay in the inception of the party itself, born in the revolutionary fervor of 1918 when left-wing radicals broke away from the Social Democratic party (SPD), the traditional political home of Germany's working class. The split destroyed the unity of the German labor movement. "For the ordinary worker," one observer noted, "it became increasingly difficult to decide which of the two parties deserved support." Former comrades, KPD and SPD members became bitter antagonists, despising each other even more than their common enemies on the right.

Hamstrung by doctrinaire orders from the Comintern in Moscow, the KPD set off on a zigzag course: It alternately tried to overthrow the hated republic by force and posed as the loyal opposition. As the nation's economy worsened in 1929, Moscow ordered the party to focus on destroying the Social Democrats, on the misbegotten notion that they, not the Nazis, represented the true "vanguard of fascism."

The decision proved suicidal. In the end, the KPD succeeded only in becoming the bogey Hitler needed to frighten voters into the arms of the National Socialists.

Communist supporters celebrate May Day 1932 beneath giant Red banners in Berlin's Lustgarten. The demonstration was ended when the Nazis provoked a riot, forcing the police to intervene.

A Communist speaker shouts invective during the 1928 May Day rally in Berlin. By this time, most independent-minded leftists had been purged from the party to make it more compliant with instructions from the Comintern.

Berlin Communists campaign from a truck adorned with the slogans "Religion is the opiate of the people" and "No higher being will save us—neither God nor kaiser nor court of justice." The KPD never won more than 17 percent of the popular vote.

Women lead a march of party faithful in Berlin. The banner at rear mocks the commander of the Reichswehr, General Hans von Seeckt, as a Nazi puppet for suppressing Red uprisings in Saxony, Thuringia, Hamburg, and the Ruhr in 1923.

Police arrest a Communist leader after a 1931 riot in which two Berlin officers were shot. Hatred between the police and the Communists ran deep; two years earlier, Karl Zörgiebel, the Social Democratic police commissioner of Berlin, had authorized his men to shoot Communists who broke the law.

pany with a youthful beauty named Geli Raubal, who was barely half his age; she was twenty and he, thirty-nine, when they began their relationship in the summer of 1928. She was also his niece, the daughter of his half sister. During the momentous events of 1929 and 1930, Hitler had kept the young woman at his side, adding a whiff of scandal to the varied ingredients of his public personality. She had, as a matter of course, been given one of the rooms in Hitler's new nine-room apartment in Munich.

By the summer of 1931, the affair had soured. Perhaps the notoriety of her famous uncle had been intriguing enough for Raubal at the beginning, but now she resented the demands Hitler made on her. With increasing desperation, she sought to regain control of her own life by resuming her study of operatic singing in the city of Vienna. Hitler would not hear of it, however, and kept her a virtual prisoner. On a September morning in 1931, as he left the apartment after a stormy argument between them, Raubal cried from a window, "Then you won't let me go to Vienna?" She received a curt no in response.

Hitler left Munich. The household staff found Geli Raubal the next day in her room, shot through the heart in what all the authorities agreed was a suicide. Hitler was devastated. Gregor Strasser later claimed that for forty-eight hours afterward, Hitler had to be prevented from taking his own life. For weeks, his grief persisted. It was during this time of personal turmoil that he was presented with his first opportunity to share power in Germany's government. He was invited to meet with Chancellor Brüning and President Hindenburg.

Neither government official had ever met with Hitler or even considered affording the Führer the recognition of a personal meeting. That they did so now was the result of Hitler's increased political stature, the desperation of the chancellor, and the behind-the-scenes maneuvering of the ubiquitous Kurt von Schleicher.

Brüning, in the midst of delicate negotiations to persuade the Allies to suspend reparations payments, was also hatching a complex plot to forestall Hitler's rise to power. Hindenburg's advanced age might force the old hero to retire from office when his term ended in 1932. In order to make sure that Hitler was denied any chance to win that powerful post, Brüning proposed the cancellation of the election, extension of the president's term of office by a vote of the Reichstag, and ultimate restoration of the monarchy. It was an improbable scheme, but the chancellor turned his full efforts to it nonetheless.

Schleicher, meanwhile, looked to control Hitler by bringing him into the government. His plan to "domesticate" Hitler, as he once put it, was as unrealistic as Brüning's. But with the confidence of a man who had not yet

On holiday in 1930, Hitler, Geli Raubal, and her mother Angela, Hitler's half sister, stand with associates on a boardwalk overlooking the North Sea. Aiming his camera at the photographer is Max Amann, the publisher of *Mein Kampf.*

met his match, Schleicher reshuffled his deck of friends and enemies and arranged to bring the president and the Nazi leader together.

Hindenburg, for his part, was trying to decide what to do with the time that was left to him. The president was eighty-four years old, and his mind and his health were failing, yet those who advised him continued to say that only he could save the country from the rising Nazi threat. Hindenburg may have agreed to spend some time with Hitler simply in order to get a look at this potential menace.

The important meetings were scheduled for October 1931. When Brüning's telegram inviting Hitler to Berlin arrived at Brown House in Munich, Hitler read it eagerly. "They have recognized me as an equal partner in negotiations," he exulted. "Now I have them in my pocket!" ✚

A motley array of early Sturmabteilung members return the salute of their squad leader. The SA recruits were to become proficient

in military drill but trained without firearms.

The Making of a Storm Trooper

"We must struggle with ideas," Hitler proclaimed, "but if necessary also with our fists." When that necessity arose, Hitler looked to a group that first displayed its muscle in 1920 as the *Sportabteilung*, or sport detachment, of the Nazi party. The innocuous title, usually abbreviated SA, furnished a convenient cover for the security guards assigned to protect Hitler and other National Socialist orators from hostile audiences. After a particularly tumultuous rally in November of 1921, when his outnumbered guards drove several hundred leftist hecklers from a Munich beer hall, a grateful Hitler assembled the SA men and renamed them his *Sturmabteilung*, or storm detachment. Henceforth, he declared, the Storm Troopers would do more than keep order at Nazi rallies; they would go on the offensive, harassing rival parties and their leaders.

To Hitler and other German army veterans of World War I, the term *Storm Trooper* evoked proud memories of the elite shock troops who had carried out fearless assaults on enemy trenches. Such hallowed associations, however, could not disguise the raw, untutored condition of many SA recruits. As the Nazi party stepped up its activities in the late 1920s and SA membership began to mushroom, more of those who donned the brown shirt were without military experience; indeed, many had never held a steady job. Transforming such footloose initiates into shock troops—even for the irregular campaigns of intimidation that Hitler had in mind—required serious training.

The first step, one SA leader explained, was to offer the recruits "what they almost always lack at home—a warm hearth, a helping hand, a sense of comradeship." Regular meals, boisterous gatherings at local taverns, and periodic bivouacs all helped foster devotion to the group. Sports and collective labor heightened that élan while working the men into fighting trim. SA chief Ernst Röhm hoped to take such regimentation a step further and mold his corps into a true army. But Hitler preferred a less provocative approach, and by and large the SA conformed to his ideal—a force sufficiently disciplined to do his bidding, yet unruly enough to inspire the masses with "wholesome fear," as Hitler put it, "and make them shudderingly submissive."

Mess tins in hand, recruits line up for a hot meal, one of the main attractions of the SA for men down on their luck.

Off-duty SA men relax in a beer hall decked with swastikas. Such taverns also served as mustering points before and after forays against rival political gangs.

Camaraderie and a Hot Meal

The SA had its own houses, hang-outs, and camps where men at loose ends found shelter and company. In return, they were on call to serve the party. "Here we learned true comradeship," a Storm Trooper said of his SA home. "During the day, we went into the villages to hand out leaflets; at night, to protect party meetings. We went from one electoral battle to the next, conquering town after town."

Trainees wash from buckets after a drill. Their annual encampments lasted up to thirty days and stressed military training, propaganda techniques, and bonding as a brotherhood of political soldiers.

SA men receive a clergyman's blessing. Early SA indoctrination paid lip service to worshiping God and attending church.

In Quest of "Strength and Dexterity"

The SA promoted sports clubs and labor service for a variety of reasons. They improved morale and attracted new members by lending the SA the healthy aura of Germany's flourishing youth organizations. SA leader Ernst Röhm considered sports and exercise good training for such specialized SA units as engineers, fliers, sailors, and alpine troops that might one day complement a full-fledged SA army. Hitler, while opposed to Röhm's objective, favored rigorous outdoor activity for the SA as a matter of principle. Through "physical strength and dexterity," he wrote, the young German "must recover his faith in the invincibility of his whole people."

SA men with digging tools set out for a day of roadwork.

Marine Youth oarsmen pull in unison.

Entrants in a 1931 SA ski meet hike to the starting point.

An SA instructor demonstrates the rudiments of gliding, a popular sport that sharpened the reflexes of future military pilots.

In a 1933 combat drill, SA recruits with mock rifles crawl beneath taut wire. The troopers were learning to keep their heads down under enemy fire.

An instructor adjusts the mask of an SA trainee wearing clothing to protect against poison gas, which both sides in World War I had used with devastating effect.

Tutelage in Mock Warfare

In January 1931, when Ernst Röhm returned from Bolivia to command the SA, his troopers signed a sweeping pledge: "I declare explicitly that I am not a member of any military unit or secret military organization, and that I have no connection to the Reichswehr or the police. I pledge that I will not participate in any military exercises."

Intended to soothe public fears about the growing strength of the SA, the oath could hardly have been more misleading. Soon after his return, Röhm and Germany's defense minister, Kurt von Schleicher, secretly agreed that in the event of war, the SA would be put under the command of the army. In return, Reichswehr training facilities were made available to SA units.

Röhm's dream was to forge a revolutionary army that would eventually overawe and absorb the tradition-bound Reichswehr. That ambition, however, put him on a collision course with Hitler.

Listening intently, SA men practice receiving electronic messages. Such training produced both military technicians and skilled operators for the Nazi party's private telegraphic and radio networks.

Enforcing the Führer's Code

The readiness of the SA to back Hitler's words with brute force had violent consequences once the party came to power. The Führer had long promised to crush Marxism in Germany, and in the weeks after he became chancellor, Storm Troopers made good on that pledge. Empowered by the thousands to bear arms as auxiliary police *(pages 102-103)*, they wreaked a final reckoning on their old adversaries of the Left.

At the same time, the SA was instrumental in dealing with the other primary target of Hitler's venom —the Jews. Early in 1933, Storm Troopers joined other Nazis to enforce a boycott of Jewish-owned businesses. There was a smattering of SS men and party officials among the uniformed pickets blocking the storefronts, but to most citizens it was the presence of the SA that mattered. Germans had learned to fear the brown shirt, and only the brave cared to cross a line held by Hitler's shock troops.

At right, an SA man plasters a shopfront with anti-Semitic slogans as an SS man *(second from right)* gestures toward the next target. Below, the SA pickets Israel's department store, one of Berlin's largest, with placards warning, "Germans, defend yourselves! Don't buy from Jews!"

An SA company (*inset*) guards the platform where a party orator speaks under a banner proclaiming, "Adolf Hitler shows you the way." Such protection was necessary; hecklers frequently charged the stage and hurled beer steins and other objects.

An SA contingent (*left*) overwhelms a Berlin police squad trying in vain to contain a Nazi demonstration in 1931. At this time, the Brownshirts were still prohibited from carrying arms.

Wounded in action, an SA street fighter receives condolences and a sprig of flowers from the Führer. Hitler vowed to strip the party insignia from any SA man who faltered in civil combat.

Giving and Taking Hard Knocks

Despite an increased emphasis on military training in the early 1930s, the mission of the SA remained primarily political. In Hitler's view, the Storm Troopers existed to forcefully carry his message to the people. As in the early days of the struggle, SA men guarded Nazi rallies, ready to wield clubs and fists against roughnecks from other parties. Brownshirts by the thousands distributed Nazi handbills and put up posters, frequently clashing with squads of communists or socialists engaged in similar activities. The sparring turned German political campaigns into bloodfests; in the month prior to the Reichstag elections of July 1932, ninety-nine partisans were killed in brawls, and hundreds more were injured.

Berlin's disgusted chief of police characterized the Storm Troopers in his city as "plain gangsters." A short time later, he discovered a pistol range at an SA hangout with a target dummy bearing his likeness. It was riddled with bullets.

Hitler demanded unflinching courage of his men and goaded them to show no mercy in their attacks. When police officials and non-Nazi newspapers deplored the brutality of the SA, Hitler was ecstatic. From such attention, he crowed, "my efforts and my party will become known, and at the same time feared."

Supervised by their chief, members of a select SA company receive their first firearms, Luger automatics, after being made auxiliary

police in 1933. In the following crackdown, Ernst Röhm boasted that his men took twelve lives for each casualty they suffered.

THREE

Maneuvering toward the Prize

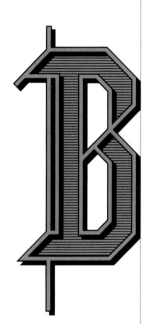

A Nazi campaign poster declares, "Our last hope: Hitler," and mirrors the crowd of Berliners gathered on a busy street corner in the depression year 1932.

arely three weeks after the suicide of his lover Geli Raubal, Adolf Hitler was summoned to Berlin for an audience with President Paul von Hindenburg. It was a momentous occasion for the Nazi leader. If he handled himself well and succeeded in winning the favor of the president, his political fortunes would soar. The meeting was just as important for the regime: If Hindenburg could win Hitler's backing, binding him to "the stake of legality," as Defense Minister Wilhelm Groener put it, the government could use the Nazi party to forge a legislative majority that would enable Germany's conservative leaders to retain power. In the process, the Nazis would be brought under control, and the threat of political paralysis—or armed revolution—averted.

Along the wide Wilhelmstrasse, near the presidential palace, a small crowd gathered on October 10, 1931, to catch a glimpse of Hitler as he passed in an open car. A few arms were raised in salute; most people in the crowd only watched and wondered. In the palace, the president waited. A staunch patriot who had served his country for more than six decades, Field Marshal Hindenburg looked foward to retirement when his official term of office ended in the spring of 1932. He had celebrated his eighty-fourth birthday on October 2 and was prone to occasional episodes of senility. He wanted nothing more than to live out his days at his country home, in the company of his Junker friends and neighbors.

But Hindenburg's long service to his nation had earned him the trust of his fellow Germans, and with trust came responsibility. Should this revered figure leave the government, it was feared, Hitler himself might run for president—and he might conceivably win. Members of Hindenburg's inner circle, therefore, had prevailed upon the old man to go along with a plan to extend his term of office. And even though Hindenburg privately scorned the upstart Nazi leader and his radical ideas, he agreed to see Hitler and attempt to win his backing.

Accompanied by Hermann Göring, Hitler met Hindenburg in his study. Even in old age, the president was an imposing figure, tall and erect, with a full head of white hair and a bushy handlebar mustache. Hitler, doubtless

affected by his recent personal tragedy, was ill at ease in the presence of this august figure, and things went wrong from the start. When the president proposed that the National Socialists support the government for the sake of the nation, Hitler responded with a harangue about the party's goals, replete with his customary oratorical flourishes. At one point, the president interrupted to reprove him for Nazi violence; Hitler then wordily promised to control his Storm Troopers. But Hindenburg was neither reassured nor impressed. When Hitler finished, the old man dismissed him with a wave of his hand. The Nazi leader offered a curt farewell and departed, with Göring at his side. Later, Hindenburg remarked contemptuously that the "Bohemian corporal" might someday become Germany's postmaster but never its chancellor—a position that only the president had the authority to fill.

On the following day, Hitler suffered another disappointment. At Bad Harzburg, a tiny mountain resort, right-wing factions had gathered to forge a coalition that would challenge the current regime. The organizer of the

Hitler addresses a rally of Nazis and German Nationalists at Bad Harzburg on October 11, 1931. At Hitler's left is the bewhiskered Nationalist leader, Alfred Hugenberg, whose conservative coalition Hitler derided as a "bourgeois mishmash."

event, Alfred Hugenberg, the publishing magnate and head of the Nationalist party, welcomed the cooperation of Hitler, a fellow dissident. Hitler agreed to attend the Harzburg rally and maintain the appearance, at least, of a united conservative front in opposition to the republican regime.

In Bad Harzburg, however, Hitler found little to his liking. For one thing, the Storm Troopers in attendance were far outnumbered by Hugenberg's Stahlhelm, or Steel Helmets, a private army made up mostly of veterans of the Great War. For another, the crowd was largely drawn from Germany's privileged classes—wealthy politicians, business people and landowners, retired generals, and even two sons of the deposed kaiser. Amid all the top hats and frock coats and bemedaled uniforms, Hitler felt very much an outsider—the custom official's son with his nose pressed against the window of money and culture.

In a dour mood, Hitler upstaged Hugenberg and shattered any notion of a united front. He called together his own forces and demanded a pledge that they follow only him. This ceremony proved lengthy and made him late for one of Hugenberg's events. Later, he dodged a meeting of the assembly's editorial committee and belittled its efforts. At the closing parade—intended to be an inspiring display of right-wing solidarity—the Führer reviewed his own troops and then immediately stalked away, snubbing the forces of the Stahlhelm. And he slighted Hugenberg further by refusing to attend a ceremonial dinner. When called to task for his belligerent behavior, Hitler explained that he could not enjoy a feast while most of his followers were out of work and hungry. Then he boasted that he led the country's largest nationalist movement and that the National Socialists would henceforth fight the Weimar government by themselves.

Putting this avowal into action, Hitler staged a large rally in the city of Braunschweig just a week after the Harzburg debacle. By train and truck he brought in 100,000 Storm Troopers and paraded them around a field for six hours, while airplanes trailing swastikas circled overhead. After sunset, the Brownshirts marched again, lighting up the night with their torches. The residents of Braunschweig were awed—as much by the way the Nazis took control of their city as by the spectacle of tens of thousands of men goose-stepping in well-ordered formations.

With the arena to himself, Hitler's high spirits returned. As he addressed his regiments at Braunschweig, he declared the Nazi movement to be "within a yard of its goal." This demonstration, he asserted, would be the last such display before the seizure of power.

The power that Hitler wanted still lay with Hindenburg and his inner circle, but as 1931 drew to a close, these men struggled to maintain their grip on the reins of government. They presided over a divided Reichstag that remained virtually paralyzed. The ten parties represented were so consumed by self-interest that they could rarely form a majority and pass a piece of legislation.

By now, the German people had lost faith in the ability of the legislative body to bring relief from the worsening woes of the depression. Nor did the executive branch of the government offer much hope. Chancellor Heinrich Brüning was an aloof, scholarly man who had tried to cope with the situation by raising taxes and lowering wages. These austerity measures, undertaken in desperation, had earned him only scorn. Disillusioned with government proposals, fearful of unrest, and tired of standing in line—for work, for food, to pawn their possessions—German citizens became increasingly vulnerable to Hitler's anti-Marxist fervor and his promises of better times to come.

No one perceived the importance of Hitler's role more clearly than Major General Kurt von Schleicher, the backstage political manipulator. Schleicher realized how dangerous it might be to leave such a man to his own devices. Hitler's brown-shirted minions now numbered in the hundreds of thousands, and their brawls with opposing groups often bordered on civil war. Throughout the autumn, Hitler himself had attacked the government in his speeches and in the press. In October, he had accused Brüning of threatening to use the army to maintain his moribund regime. Two months later, in response to a radio broadcast in which the chancellor appealed to Germans to refrain from devisive criticism of the government, the Nazi leader charged Brüning with attempting to curtail freedom of speech. "You yourself, Herr Chancellor, jealously see to it that only the government is permitted liberty of action in Germany," he wrote. "What then, Herr Chancellor, remains for us but speech to bring to the knowledge of the German nation our views on the ruinous character of your plans, or the errors that underlie them and the disasters that must ensue?"

Schleicher was in a position to do something about this ominous situation. As head of the Ministry Bureau of the Reichswehr, an arm of Groener's defense establishment, he served as chief liaison between the military and other ministries; he had also used the army's intelligence system to plant informers in every government office. His appearance was unimpressive—he was short and balding and bulged slightly at the waist —but he was a gifted political strategist who, in the words of one of his colleagues, "could get along with everyone." He had the ear of President Hindenburg and was on intimate terms with Groener, who looked on him as an adopted son. Thus Schleicher spent much of his time on Wilhelmstrasse, surreptitiously arranging government affairs. Those who knew him

At Home with the "Iron Hindenburg"

After almost half a century of military service, General Paul von Hindenburg had enjoyed barely three years of retirement when the guns of August 1914 summoned him to the eastern front. Within weeks, the Eighth Army, led by the sixty-seven-year-old Hindenburg and his chief of staff Erich Ludendorff, destroyed two Russian armies at Tannenberg and Masurian Lakes. Overnight, the Iron Hindenburg—as phlegmatic as he was courageous—became a national hero. In 1916, he was named chief of the general staff, and he oversaw Germany's last offensives and eventual retreat in the West.

Admired even in defeat, Hindenburg guided the army home and resumed the life of an aristocratic old soldier. In 1925, however, duty lured him from retirement once more, this time to become president of the nation that idolized him still.

Paul von Hindenburg and his life-size portrait dominate a salon in his East Prussian home.

Neudeck *(left)*, the estate presented to the Hindenburg family by Frederick the Great, had passed into creditors' hands. But the president's supporters bought the place, restored its elegance *(below)*, and gave it to him on his birthday in 1927.

Hindenburg and his grandchildren stroll a tree-lined avenue leading from the presidential palace in Berlin.

The squire of Neudeck entertains his *Kamarilla*, or inner circle, in 1932. Seated clockwise from left are Chancellor Papen, State Secretary Otto Meissner, Hindenburg, Defense Minister Schleicher, and Interior Minister Wilhelm von Gayl.

A dedicated hunter, Hindenburg and a young companion display a pair of antelopes bagged on an outing in the Bavarian Alps.

best sensed that Schleicher simply enjoyed political maneuvering and particularly liked to watch careers rise and fall at his behest. Indeed, he was perfectly defined by his last name, which meant schemer.

Schleicher never wavered in his resolve to win Hitler over and use him and the Nazi party to form a powerful conservative coalition that would dominate the Reichstag. Schleicher also coveted the SA as a valuable source of trained personnel—a national militia that could support the under-strength Reichswehr against such potential enemies as Poland and France. So as the cold gray German winter began, he pressured the government to summon the "Bohemian corporal" once again.

Hitler received the telegram in Munich. Jubilant, he hastened to the capital and installed himself in the Kaiserhof, a large hotel where the party now had its Berlin headquarters—diagonally across the street from the chancellery and the presidential palace.

The government's request was more specific than it had been in the autumn: Would Hitler ask the National Socialist members of the Reichstag to approve an extension of the president's term without an election? In return, Brüning would resign in a year or two—after he had set Germany's foreign affairs in order and put the economy on the road to recovery—and Brüning himself might recommend Hitler for the chancellorship.

Hitler had worked too hard in the past decade, however, to risk his influence on a hazy gentleman's agreement, and the notion of sharing power was abhorrent to him. Still, for more than a week he consulted his lieutenants back at the Hotel Kaiserhof and mulled over the proposal. Only Gregor Strasser urged him to accept the offer; Joseph Goebbels and Ernst Röhm argued vehemently against it. Goebbels noted in his diary that "everyone is scuttling about on Wilhelmstrasse like a lot of distracted hens. It is we who hold all the cards."

Finally, in mid-January of 1932, Hitler replied to the government's request. Ever flexible in tactical matters, he now presented himself as a staunch defender of the constitution. The proposal to extend the president's term without an election, he declared, was a breach of this document. If the president renounced the scheme, then Hitler would offer his support in a legal election. Of course, Brüning would have to go, and there had to be new Reichstag elections as well.

Not surprisingly, the government refused to consider these stipulations, and it became clear to Hitler that his only recourse was to run for president himself. Still, unwilling to commit himself to a campaign against so formidable an opponent, he vacillated. Hindenburg also seemed uncertain of his next move. Meanwhile, tension mounted in Nazi party ranks. "Everyone is nervous and overstrung," noted Goebbels.

While weighing his chances, Hitler kept busy. Toward the end of January, he wrote to Brüning two times, harshly censuring the chancellor for advocating a breach of the constitution and warning that the current legislature, which had been seated more than a year earlier, no longer represented popular sentiment and could not legally vote to continue the president's term. After delivering these jabs, he left for Düsseldorf, a major industrial center in the western part of the republic. There, in the ballroom of the Park Hotel, he addressed a sizable gathering of the Industry Club, an organization of business executives, sales representatives, trade-association officials, and corporate lawyers. The speech, like all of Hitler's public oratory, was ingeniously tailored to fit the audience, to play on its fears, hatreds, and hopes.

For these merchants and magnates, Hitler lambasted both representative

government and communism. Democracy, he explained, was promoted as the rule of the people but in reality was "the rule of stupidity, of mediocrity, of halfheartedness, of cowardice, of weakness, and of inadequacy." Furthermore, the rule of the many could only lead to economic ruin, for in a democratically run country, communism would inevitably take over industry. And if bolshevism were not stopped, predicted the Führer in his pinstriped suit, it would overrun the globe, transforming the world "as completely as Christianity did in times past."

Speaking for more than two hours, Hitler touched on many other areas of Nazi philosophy—scrupulously avoiding, however, any mention of its anti-Jewish precepts, since there were likely to be Jews in the ballroom. He did discuss the "supremacy" of the white race and offer the notion that the "inner value of a people" depended on its racial purity—its "blood-conditioned composition." The potent Germany of earlier days, he maintained, had drawn its strength from the "sense of lordship of the so-called Nordic man."

Toward the end of his discourse, Hitler spoke of his own humble beginnings in politics. In 1918, he said, he had recognized the need to found a new organization to piece together the wrecked German nation. The endeavor would be a struggle, he had realized, because of his modest origins: "I was only a nameless German soldier, with a very small zinc identification number on my breast." He boasted of founding the party with six other men—although, in reality, he had joined the tiny cell some time after its inception—and lauded the outcome of their efforts. "Today, that movement cannot be destroyed," he declared. "People must reckon with it whether they like it or not."

The oratory was brilliant, but Hitler offered little in the way of practical suggestions for economic recovery. Big business remained leery of the word *socialist* in the party's name and viewed the Nazis as political agitators—little better than rabble. The business people listening to Hitler at Düsseldorf and those who heard him on subsequent occasions donated only small sums to the Nazi cause. The party would continue to be financed largely by its membership dues and the admission fees—some of them exorbitant—charged at giant rallies.

After the Düsseldorf speech, Hitler checked into Brown House in Munich, where he and Goebbels discussed plans for a presidential campaign. Still, no announcement of Hitler's candidacy was made, and the tension

In a misperception shared by many, this 1932 cartoon in the Social Democrats' party weekly depicts Hitler as a pawn of self-satisfied business tycoons.

continued. "One has to keep one's nerve and know how to wait," wrote Goebbels. Finally, on February 15, Hindenburg announced his candidacy. A week later, Goebbels proclaimed to a mob at Berlin's Sportpalast that the Nazi party would declare Adolf Hitler as its candidate for Reich president.

With the elections only three weeks away, the Nazi propaganda machinery, already well oiled and running smoothly, whirred into overdrive. Early in 1931, Hitler had organized the Reichspropagandaleitung (RPL), or Reich Propaganda Directorate, which was in charge of dispersing the Nazi message. The tentacles of the RPL stretched into all parts of Germany, from major cities such as Berlin, Munich, and Hamburg, to tiny villages such as Dietramszell, the country hamlet where Hindenburg based his autumn hunting trips. Each month, the RPL sent all gauleiters, or district party leaders, directives outlining the propaganda campaign for the next thirty days. In return, the gauleiters polled public opinion in their areas and submitted monthly summaries to the RPL, which then used this information to develop its themes. There was a message for everyone, from women to civil servants to blue-collar workers, and the gauleiters were encouraged to select the themes best suited to the local populations.

The central weapon in the Nazi propaganda arsenal, however, was the mass meeting. During the three-week campaign for the presidency, the party staged an astounding 300 meetings a day in cities and towns across Germany. Hitler, Goebbels, and Strasser traversed the country in order to speak at the largest of the rallies, which took place in flag-draped halls lined with Storm Troopers. Their speeches were full of catch phrases. "We stand at the turning point of Germany's destiny," Hitler would cry from the flower-laden podium. "We fight today! We fight tomorrow!" The direction in which the Nazis intended to steer was vague; nonetheless, the torrent of words and the emotional delivery intoxicated the crowds. Soon, Hitler promised, life itself would once more take on meaning and purpose, and the German people would again feel "joy in their hearts."

To intensify the fervor incited by such speeches, towns were papered with posters, littered with leaflets, and treated to the spectacle of SA legions in the streets singing "Germany, Awake!" Fifty thousand recordings of campaign rhetoric were cut, and the Nazi message blared from loudspeakers mounted on trucks. There were even Nazi propaganda movies; their sheer novelty was enough to draw crowds in the towns and villages. Most of the campaign rhetoric—spoken, printed, recorded, filmed—could be distilled to a single message: "Adolf Hitler is our last hope."

Local party leaders worked hard to win votes. They provided soup kitchens, backed public-assistance measures, and launched other relief campaigns for the poor. The Nazis also won converts by sponsoring professional and trade organizations such as the Fighting Association of German Architects and the Fighting League of Militant Retailers. Membership in one such organization, the Nazi trade union for industrial workers, grew from 39,000 in 1931 to 400,000 in 1933. And when the Nazis could not supplant an existing organization, they infiltrated it.

In opposition to this political dynamo, Chancellor Brüning mounted a spirited campaign on Hindenburg's behalf. He, too, spoke at packed meeting halls across Germany, eulogizing the president. Hindenburg participated directly only twice: He allowed a short film to be made of his declaration of candidacy, and, toward the end of the campaign, he broadcast a radio message to the nation. Warning against the grave dangers of a "party man" with "one-sided, extremist views," he expressed his fears for Germany should Hitler gain office. Hindenburg considered it his clear duty to prevent this. "If I am defeated," the old field marshal humbly told the country, "at least I will not have incurred the reproach that of my own accord I deserted my post in an hour of crisis. I ask for no votes from those who do not wish to vote for me."

When the ballots were counted, Hindenburg had fallen half a percentage point short of a majority. To prove his right to continue as the nation's leader, he would have to endure another election. The Nazi candidate had received just over 30 percent of the total, roughly 11 million votes. The result was far less than a mandate, but almost twice the Nazi tally in the Reichstag election a year and a half earlier. The remainder of the votes were unevenly shared by candidates of the Nationalist and Communist parties. In a radical departure from the past, many of those who now voted for Hitler were Junkers, the landed aristocrats who in more settled times would have cast their lot with Hindenburg. Thus the president emerged as the choice of the moderate socialists, the Catholic center, and the trade unions—uncomfortable company for the stubborn monarchist.

Despite their huge gains, the Nazis were not entirely happy either. They were still far from achieving a majority; in Berlin, in fact, only 23 percent of the voters had supported them. Just as demoralizing was the prospect of another campaign, this one to be financed from empty coffers and run by a tired, disappointed crew. In his private moments, even Hitler revealed his frustration. A party member who visited the Führer's unlit apartment late one night found him to be "the image of a disappointed, discouraged gambler who had wagered beyond his means."

Publicly, however, Hitler showed no sign of flagging. "He does not hesitate to face the fight once more," wrote Goebbels. "I have never seen him waver." Party members took the lead. The editor of the *Völkischer Beobachter*, Alfred Rosenberg, penned the party line: "Now the fight goes on

In an era when most people had never flown, Hitler barnstormed incessantly. *Below:* During the 1932 presidential campaign, Hitler studies his itinerary with his aide and flying companion, Wilhelm Brückner. *Bottom:* An SS honor guard meets the Führer at an airfield in East Prussia.

with a fierceness, a ruthlessness, that Germany has never experienced before. The basis of our struggle is hatred for everything that opposes us."

For this second round, Hitler and his men added a novel tactic, one born of necessity. Fearing for the country's stability, Chancellor Brüning had halted all electioneering until after Easter. This left only a week of campaigning before the runoff on April 10. To make the most of the time, the Nazis chartered a Ju 52 passenger plane from Lufthansa to carry Hitler and his escort from border to border. They called the campaign "Hitler over Germany," and in the course of a week, the Führer touched down in twenty-one cities—on one occasion, he even took off in a violent storm that had grounded most flights. This kind of courage, the Nazis pointed out, was exactly what Germany needed.

Thanks to the frantic campaigning, Hitler on election day added about two million votes to his March total. But the dogged persistence of the Nazis was not enough to win the prize. Hin-

Den letzten Stoß! Liste **2**

National-Soz-Deutsche-Arbeiter-Partei N.S.D.A.P.

Mehr Macht dem Reichspräsidenten!

Weg mit der Alleinherrschaft der Parlamente (Artifel 54) Wählt Deutschnational

KPD LISTE 3

Schluss mit diesem System

On a float declaring "Hindenburg stays!" campaigners representing the middle class—from soldier to cook to transit worker—appeal to Berliners in 1932. In the posters above (*from left to right*), Nazis aim a blow at Catholics and Communists, Nationalists urge a strong president to quell the Reichstag, and Communists demand an end to the system. Opposite, the Social Democrats predict the workers' fate under the Nazis, and the People's party warns of inflation and civil war.

denburg, who picked up fewer than one million additional supporters, nevertheless obtained the majority that he required to remain in office.

Once again, Hitler had been thwarted at the polls. But events behind the scenes were now conspiring to radically alter the political situation—and achieve for Hitler what no amount of campaigning could do. The question of how to deal with the SA was central to this unfolding drama. By the spring of 1932, membership in the Brownshirts had swollen to 400,000—four times the size of the Reichswehr. Police in several cities had found evidence that SA leaders, apparently acting on their own, had made contingency plans to seize power locally. The provincial governments of Prussia and Bavaria, hard-pressed to maintain order in the streets, beseeched the central government to do something about the Nazi army. The appeals were addressed to Defense Minister Groener, who had been given additional duties as minister of the interior. Now responsible for internal order, Groener asked the government to act, and on April 13, three days after Hindenburg was reelected, the cabinet banned all uniformed organizations of the Nazi party, including the SS, the Führer's black-shirted protection squad. Police occupied the shelters and depots where Hitler's troops had gathered to plot their riots and brawls.

The Storm Troopers were forced underground for the time being, but Hitler seemed undaunted. He enthusiastically campaigned for his party in a round of local and state elections in Prussia, Bavaria, Anhalt, Württemberg. Four-fifths of all Germans would go to the polls on April 24, 1932. By now, Hitler had emerged as a major figure whose appearances were guaranteed to attract the curious as well as the committed. His oratory was at its peak, and his performances were brilliantly orchestrated to capture the imagination of his listeners. Whenever possible, he spoke at night; during the day, he felt, he could not establish the necessary bond with his audience. Building suspense was also part of the program, and Hitler would keep his throngs waiting, sometimes for hours. When he finally appeared at the podium, bathed in a bright light, he would pause to take the measure of the crowd. Only when he had determined the mood of an evening would he launch into speech, leading his rapt audience, step by step, to a frenzy of emotion, releasing them only with his final words. By the end of his oration, Hitler's shirt would be soaked in sweat, and he would be exhausted. As the crowd cheered, he would exit the arena and retreat to his hotel room, where he would frequently sip vegetable soup in silence.

In this manner, Hitler covered twenty-six towns in late April. The results were equivocal. In Prussia, the largest German state, the party netted roughly the same percentage of the electorate that Hitler himself had won in the presidential runoff. Elsewhere, the percentage was smaller, but the Nazi party did gain delegates to local legislatures. It was enough to keep the Weimar regime on edge.

While Hitler was campaigning that spring, the master schemer Kurt von Schleicher started a campaign of his own, aimed at disposing of key members of Hindenburg's cabinet. Schleicher began by changing his stance on the ban of the SA and SS. The political general had at first backed the prohibition, but almost before it was instituted he secretly met with Hitler to assure him that he opposed the injunction. And Schleicher soon pressured President Hindenburg to lift the ban. Otherwise, Schleicher argued, the government should also surpress the Reichsbanner, the pro-republic militant arm of the Social Democrats.

Meanwhile, Schleicher maligned his old mentor Groener, whom he now saw as a pawn of the Social Democrats and an impediment to dealing with Hitler. Schleicher turned the leading generals against the defense minister and sowed the seeds of distrust in the fading mind of the eighty-four-year-old Hindenburg. Schleicher used his close relationship with Oskar von Hindenburg, the president's son and personal aide, to gain the old man's confidence. Schleicher spread rumors and made jokes under his breath about Groener's infant son, who had been born only five months after the wedding vows were spoken. Finally, he delivered the coup de grâce by icily informing Groener that he no longer enjoyed the confidence of the army. On May 12, after enduring days of scalding invective from the Nazi delegates in the Reichstag, Groener resigned as defense minister.

Having dispatched Groener, Schleicher set out to steamroller Brüning, whom he saw as the next obstacle in his path. Publicly, he supported the chancellor as "the only one who can master the situation in Germany in the foreseeable future." However, when the chancellor requested that Schleicher take the defense post Groener had just vacated, the inveterate schemer replied, "I will, but not in your government." Schleicher spent the second half of May turning Hindenburg against Brüning, a task made easier by the president's mood. Far from being grateful for the chancellor's loyal campaigning in March and April, Hindenburg instead bore a grudge against Brüning. He felt the chancellor had exposed him to a contentious election in which he had been associated with the leftist factions that he and his conservative colleagues loathed.

Some of these same supporters had engineered the purchase of the Hindenburg-family estate, Neudeck, and presented it to the president. He was now enjoying the fine spring weather there. While they had Hindenburg's ear, the Junkers made it clear that they, too, wanted Brüning removed from office. Aware of Hindenburg's prejudice, Schleicher confidently planned for a new government to replace Brüning and his cabinet. Meanwhile, he met with Hitler and proposed a deal: The new administration would lift the ban on the Nazis' paramilitary units and would hold new Reichstag elections in exchange for Hitler's tacit support—which he need offer only temporarily.

Late in May, Hindenburg returned to Berlin. At a meeting on May 29, Brüning found the president's mood unusually cool. Presented with a batch of decrees to sign, Hindenburg responded evasively; he said he preferred to discuss the issues with other government leaders. Furthermore, the president complained, Brüning's government was far too liberal; he had heard that some ministers even had bolshevist leanings. Dismayed, Brüning asked if the president wanted him to resign; the answer was yes.

Late that same day, votes were tallied in another state election, this one in Oldenburg, in the northwestern corner of Germany. For the first time, the Nazis had won a majority in a local legislature. The election results reverberated in Berlin. While many in the capital held their breath awaiting news of the chancellorship, there were rumblings that a Nazi takeover was imminent. Students arriving at one Berlin school on the day after the election found a Nazi flag waving from the roof. When the janitor refused to open the door to the tower from which the banner fluttered, one of the teachers, a veteran who had lost his left arm in the Great War, climbed out of a dormer window and crawled across the roof to pull down the flag.

Later that morning, three pupils in Nazi uniforms complained about the teacher; the principal of the school promised a "careful investigation" of the charges and suspended the one-armed veteran. Someone scrawled an anti-Semitic slogan on the blackboard in his classroom. And when school was dismissed at midday for lunch, members of the Hitler Youth attacked a twelve-year-old Jewish boy, beating him until they were chased off by their outraged classmates.

Ominous as the incident was, the young Nazis were premature in flaunting triumph. The new chancellor, who took office on June 1, 1932, was not Hitler but Franz von Papen, a fifty-three-year-old right-wing aristocrat. Papen lacked the confidence and support of any political party. He was described by a contemporary as a man who "enjoyed the peculiarity of being taken seriously by neither his friends nor his enemies." Schleicher knew this, of course. When he was accused of selecting a chancellor with no head for the job, he replied, "I don't need a head, I need a hat." Although Papen showed no particular brilliance, he was charming, wealthy, and socially well connected. It would not be long before this rather pompous flatterer would insinuate himself into the confidence of the weary presi-

Furnishings from an SA headquarters are stacked in a truck
after elections in April 1932.
To avert a Brownshirt coup, the
Brüning government outlawed
the SA and SS and ordered their
offices and barracks stripped.

JA-15821

dent—who took to calling Papen, thirty years his junior, by the friendly diminutive "Franzchen."

Every member of the new cabinet was chosen by Schleicher, who took the post of defense minister for himself. All of the appointees seemed cut in the mold of Papen—rich, aristocratic, conservative, and, since they had no political base, largely ineffective. Together, they were contemptuously called the "cabinet of barons."

In his first act as chancellor, Papen politely requested that Adolf Hitler guarantee in writing his party's support for the new government. Instead, Hitler demanded action on Schleicher's promises to stage new Reichstag elections and to allow the SA and SS to resume their activities. By mid-June, Papen conceded both points; in return, he was assured—orally—that the Nazis would cooperate with his regime. In reality, however, the party taunted the chancellor by marching its uniformed troops in public before the ban was officially lifted. Hitler was determined not to become associated in the public mind with Papen and his enervated "cabinet of barons." As propaganda chief Goebbels put it, "If we let ourselves be made responsible for their doings, we shall lose all our chances."

The behavior of the SA in the weeks following the end of the ban provided, for the German people, a stark contrast to the government's lethargy. For two months, the restive troops had been forced to check their emotions. Now, with the floodgate open, they rampaged as never before. Wield-

Mounted police break up a demonstration in Munich protesting the prohibition of the SA and SS. When Chancellor Brüning was ousted two months later, the ban was lifted.

Police use a water cannon atop an armored truck to quench renewed street-fighting in the summer of 1932. After reinstatement by Papen, which the communists called "an invitation to murder," the SA ran wild; in five weeks, 133 Nazis, communists, and police were killed.

ing blackjacks, brass knuckles, and *Stahlruten*—short open pipes containing spring-loaded steel balls—gangs of Nazi toughs clashed with the angry forces of the Left. Daily street battles raged throughout the nation. In Prussia, the toll after five weeks was ninety-nine dead and ten times that many wounded. The violence crested on Sunday, July 17, two weeks before the Reichstag elections. In the fishing port of Altona, in Hamburg, a Nazi force 7,000 strong invaded a working-class neighborhood. Communist snipers fired from roofs and windows, and Storm Troopers returned the fire. When the battle ended, seventeen more Germans lay dead.

This bloodshed gave Papen an opening he sought. It turned out that the new chancellor had his own ideas about governing and for some weeks had been contemplating action against the Prussian state government. With its capital at Berlin, Prussia contained three-fifths of the German population and was the last major stronghold of the Social Democratic party. Control of its government would place immense power in the hands of the conservatives. Besides, as a new man in office, Papen needed to demonstrate his potency, lest he too become a scapegoat like Brüning.

Accordingly, Papen obtained a presidential decree allowing him to remove the Prussian government from office and place the state under the Reich's administration. For an excuse, he cited the riot at Altona as evidence that the Prussian leaders could no longer guarantee law and order in their own jurisdiction.

On July 20, the chancellor set his coup in motion. Wisely, he chose a time when the Prussian premier was not in Berlin. The local government put up only perfunctory resistance, and, before forty-eight hours had passed, Papen had seized control of the state and its police force of 85,000. The most vocal protest came from a small band of police who had gathered in support of Berlin's police commissioner, Albert Grzesinski. As the senior police officers were led into internment, the little group called out, *"Freiheit!"* (freedom)—the Social Democrats' answer to "Heil Hitler!"

On the heels of Papen's coup came the Reichstag elections. Again the Nazis campaigned hard, playing on the anxieties of the depression-plagued population. The Nazi propaganda machine customized its messages to appeal to a variety of factions. To those on pensions that had shrunk during the depression, the party pledged the "revalorization of savings and just and adequate retirement care." To civil servants, whose salaries had been slashed as one of Brüning's austerity measures, the Nazis vowed to "reestablish the rights that have been taken from the civil service"—and, incidentally, to remove "all members of the Jewish race" from government payrolls. And the Nazis placed new emphasis on wooing the traditionally left-wing workers. Posters advertising *Arbeit und Brot*—work and bread—and speeches swearing "the participation of the working class in the ownership of property" appealed to the unemployed in this group.

This time, the Nazi campaign paid dividends. In the new Reichstag, the sixth since 1919, Nazis gained 230 of the 608 seats, a total that often fluctuated from election to election. Though short of a majority, they had nearly 100 more votes than the Social Democrats, the next-largest delegation. More than 13 million Germans cast ballots for the Nazis. Clearly, the party had become a haven for the disappointed and apprehensive of almost every caste. These people now looked on their splintered republic with contempt. By contrast, when they saluted Hitler, their eyes shone.

After the Nazi success in the Reichstag elections, the conservatives needed Hitler more than ever. The country's lawmaking mechanism had all but ceased to function. In 1930, the Reichstag had passed ninety-eight laws. But in 1931, only thirty-four acts had survived the process, and the record was worsening. At the same time, Hindenburg was bypassing the Reichstag and enacting so-called emergency decrees simply by signing his name to them. Although the constitution permitted this procedure, Hindenburg was publishing edicts at an unprecedented rate—five per month. The government, propped up by the bayonets of the Reichswehr, ruled with almost no popular support. It was a volatile situation that might lead to insurrection—especially now that one voter in three subscribed to the corrosive

Nazi doctrine. Unsurprisingly, the government pushed once more for a reconciliation with the Führer.

In early August, Hitler met with Schleicher, who still believed he could manipulate the Nazi leader to his advantage. This time, Hitler demanded the chancellorship for himself and a guarantee of four cabinet positions for his party. He would also require the establishment of a new government agency, the Ministry of Popular Enlightenment and Propaganda. Furthermore, he wished to have his own men installed at the head of the Prussian government. Schleicher did not blanch. Although no decision was reached, Hitler left the parley in high spirits. As he bade the general farewell, he suggested that a plaque be mounted on the house where they had met, commemorating the event.

Hitler went to his retreat near Berchtesgaden to await the government's reply; Schleicher departed for Neudeck to discuss the Nazi leader's conditions with Hindenberg. In the streets, increasingly frequent vandalism and political murder prompted Hindenburg to sign yet another decree, this one authorizing the death sentence for political assassins. As if on cue, five SA men in the Upper Silesian village of Potempa broke into the home of a communist miner, Konrad Pietrzuch, on August 10. In full view of his mother, they beat and stomped the hapless man to death. That day in Bavaria, where Goebbels waited with Hitler, the Nazi chronicler noted a meteor shower. "A lovely evening closes in over the Obersalzberg," he wrote. "Falling stars shower down from the sky like golden rain."

Franz von Papen, considered a better horseman than statesman, was surprised when offered the chancellorship in May 1932. "I doubt very much," he said, "if I am the right man."

A few days later, Hitler returned to Berlin for a meeting with Schleicher and Papen. On his way to the capital, the Führer brimmed with confidence. While eating a piece of cake in a restaurant, he described to his escort his plans to massacre the Marxists once he gained power. At his meeting on Wilhelmstrasse, he was told that Hindenburg, by this time quite fond of "Franzchen," would offer Hitler no more than the vice chancellorship. Thwarted again, Hitler raged at the two men: He would wipe out the Marxists; he would unleash the SA; thousands would die.

Schleicher later commented that the Nazi leader seemed to have gone insane. But to Goebbels, who joined Hitler for lunch after the meeting, the Führer's wrath was merely a sign that he stood "firm and resolute."

In the afternoon, Hitler was summoned to speak with Hindenburg. The Führer went, hoping the president had reconsidered. But the stubborn old field marshal had no intention of surrendering to the former lance corporal. Coolly but courteously, Hindenburg explained that he welcomed Nazi participation but would not yield full power to one party. Only recently, he reminded Hitler, the National Socialists had agreed to support the Papen regime. A coalition government that included the Nazis was acceptable to him, he went on, but he "could not take the responsibility of giving power to Hitler alone."

Chancellor Papen leaves a polling place after voting in the Reichstag elections of July 31, 1932. Party workers at the entrance wear signs indicating the ballot number of their party.

Having tasted disappointment twice in one day, Hitler returned to Goebbels's apartment only to find a few more sour drops left for him to swallow. The afternoon newspapers were already full of the government's version of the discussion, and, under headlines such as "Hitler Reprimanded by the Reich President," the press portrayed a Nazi defeat.

Perhaps because of his lingering bitterness, Hitler now committed a tactical mistake that would cost him popularity. On August 22, the Brownshirts who had ruthlessly murdered the communist miner were sentenced to death. Hitler threw his lot in with the murderers. "I feel bound to you in limitless loyalty," he telegraphed. "It is our duty to fight against a government that could allow this."

While entertaining guests on the veranda of his villa on the Obersalzberg at the end of August, Hitler attempted to justify his stance on the case. One of his visitors was the Nazi Hermann Rauschning, president of the senate of Danzig, a German city under League of Nations control. Rauschning was surprised by the Führer's surroundings. There were songbirds in cages, elderly matrons in attendance, and a generally petit-bourgeois ambiance. This was odd, Rauschning thought: Although Hitler courted shopkeepers and artisans, he privately decried the values of the middle class.

In the Salzburg Alps, Hitler alternated between morose silence and frantic commentary. He spoke passionately of the need to commit cruelties with a "clear conscience," as his Storm Troopers had done in trampling the miner to death. Only by such radical acts, he said, "can we expel our nation's softheartedness and sentimental philistinism."

"We have no time for fine feelings," the Führer continued. "We must compel our nation to greatness if it is to fulfill its historic task." Germany's mission, of course, involved a war. Hitler envisioned it as nearly bloodless. "The place of artillery preparation for frontal attack will in the future be taken by revolutionary propaganda," he explained. In this way, he would conquer the enemy's psyche before his armies needed to fire their guns. "How to achieve the moral breakdown of the enemy before the war has started—that is the problem that interests me." Yet Hitler was also considering the possibility of failure. At one point, he asked Rauschning about the right of asylum in Danzig, where German law did not apply. He thought he might flee there if he needed to go underground.

In Berlin, Papen, too, was preparing for the worst when the new Reichstag—packed with 230 Nazi delegates—convened on September 12. Toward the end of August, he journeyed to Hindenburg's country estate, Neudeck, where he found the president sunning himself on the terrace. Papen obtained from Hindenburg a decree authorizing him to dissolve the leg-

islature at any time a majority threatened a vote to oust the government.

When the new Reichstag met, Papen was forearmed. On its first day, the legislature was asked to consider a motion to dismiss Papen and his ministers. Göring, who had been elected Reichstag president, called for the voting. Intending to preempt the motion by dissolving the legislature, Papen immediately stood to be recognized. With a smirk, however, Göring turned away and continued the vote. Papen stalked angrily to the podium, flung the dissolution decree in front of Göring, and walked out, accompanied by his ministers. Facing the empty chairs where the cabinet had sat, ten delegates voted no confidence in the government for each one who supported it. Yet a slender thread held Germany to its constitution: Because of Papen's dissolution decree, the Reichstag vote was deemed illegal. The nation would face another election—the fourth in less than a year.

At a dramatic moment in the Nazi-led Reichstag, Chancellor Papen (*standing at left center*) seeks recognition from Hermann Göring (*upper right*); the Reichstag president ignored him and held a vote of no confidence in Papen's government.

The Nazis did not welcome the new election. They had run a concerted campaign in July and won. Subsequent events—the murder trial of the SA men, Hitler's outspoken approval of their atrocity, the embarrassing publicity over his meeting with Hindenburg—had alienated voters. Just as troubling was a lack of cash in the party coffers. "The party exchequer is empty," wrote Goebbels in mid-September.

With what resources they had left, the Nazis fired up their propaganda machine once again and distributed speeches, newspaper articles, leaflets, and posters. Again the Führer took to the skies in his now-familiar flights over Germany. The Nazis lambasted the government as the "clique of nobles" and the "corrupt Junker regime." At the same time, their propaganda courted the working class with proposals to replace the present form of government with one vaguely based on socialism; a Nazi slogan offered an "honest living for honest work." And a few days before the election, Hitler allowed party members to join their old enemies, the communists, in support of Berlin's striking transport workers. The resulting work stoppage raised the specter of a totalitarian coalition of Nazis and communists—a vision that horrified the conservatives.

Despite their efforts, the Nazis' fortunes were reversed on November 6. They lost thirty-four Reichstag seats, while rival parties, particularly the conservatives, gained. The losses were no fluke; in local elections a week later, support for Hitler also edged downward. By attempting to attract the working class, the Nazis had alienated many of their conservative supporters. Despite its surface frenzy, the campaign had lacked energy as well as funds. By this time the German people, too, were worn out, exhausted by the emotional rhetoric of the previous eight months.

As 1932 drew to a close, the struggle for power continued amid fresh intrigues. Defense Minister Schleicher decided to depose Chancellor Papen. Papen had proved less tractable than Schleicher had hoped. In fact, he showed signs of wanting to rule as a virtual dictator, and as long as he remained in office, there was little hope that the government could come to terms with the Nazis. Schleicher went to Hindenburg and whispered in his ear: Papen's autocratic tendencies, he said, threatened to trigger violent reactions from both the communists and the Nazis—revolts that even the army would not be able to quell. Hindenburg listened to his defense minister, and on December 1, Papen unhappily resigned his post. The wily Schleicher was appointed the new chancellor.

As part of his latest scheme, Schleicher had attempted to drive a wedge through the Nazi party by courting Hitler's main ideological rival, Gregor Strasser, and offering to share power with the Nazis. Strasser seemed

willing to deal with the new chancellor, but when Hitler learned of the negotiations, he erupted in fury. On December 5, he and Strasser quarreled violently in the Führer's quarters at the Hotel Kaiserhof. Hitler was adamant; only he had the right to power, and only he would negotiate with the government. Two days later, during another blistering exchange at the Kaiserhof, Hitler accused Strasser of treachery. This time, Strasser retreated to his room and drafted a letter of resignation from his party post. He wrote sadly of his loyalty and his longstanding dream—now smashed—of a coalition of forward-looking men who would govern Germany.

Although Strasser signed his letter "constantly yours truly," he failed to mention what plans he might have for the sizable contingent of party members under his sway. Hitler despaired, half expecting Strasser to pull out his supporters and wreck the party. For hours he paced anxiously in his suite, pausing once to threaten suicide "if the party falls to pieces." But Strasser's loyalty held. He left town quietly and took his family to Austria for a canoeing vacation. Nonetheless, the party had lost its momentum. In mid-December Goebbels wrote, "It is high time we attain power, although for the moment there is not the slightest chance of it." And two days before Christmas, as he pondered the future, he saw only darkness and gloom—"All chances have quite disappeared."

Hitler, too, was grim. In a thank-you note to an old friend, he wrote, "I have given up all hope. Nothing will ever come of my dreams." Again the Führer mentioned suicide: "As soon as I am sure that everything is lost you know what I will do. I cannot accept defeat. I will stick to my word and end my life with a bullet."

As had happened in times past, however, events now conspired to give Hitler a new lease on life. Papen began a campaign to overthrow his nemesis, Schleicher. On January 4, 1933, Papen traveled to Cologne for a top-secret meeting with Hitler to propose that the two forge a coalition of the Nationalist and National Socialist parties and lead it jointly. Although the two reached no agreement that day, they parted on good terms—as Schleicher and Hitler had the previous summer. Papen convinced himself that his Nazi co-conspirator was becoming more flexible.

Whatever else the meeting may have been, it was a source of fresh strength for Hitler and the Nazis, and it dispelled the depression that had overtaken the party in December. His spirits renewed, Hitler threw himself into an election campaign in Lippe, a tiny state with a population of only 100,000. He was determined to win a victory that would call attention to Nazi potency. In only a few days, Hitler spoke at sixteen rallies, and Goebbels and other party principals also performed tirelessly. Their efforts

In an unusual instance of cooperation, Nazi and Communist flags supporting a rent strike fly side by side in a Berlin workers' neighborhood late in 1932. The message scrawled across the far wall reads, "Food first, then rent."

Lights and torches illuminate the Brandenburg Gate on January 29, 1933 as 25,000 marchers acclaim Hitler's elevation to chancellor. Goebbels decreed it "the night of the great miracle."

were successful; the Nazis garnered 39.5 percent of the votes, their first clear success since the July sweep. The party press proclaimed a landslide and predicted the passing of power to the Führer.

Papen was doing his best to make the prediction come true. Obsessed with the desire to form an alliance with Hitler, he was now willing to help the Nazi leader become chancellor. But one gigantic obstacle remained—the president. Hindenburg's distrust of the Nazis, his entrenched resistance to one-party rule, and his distaste for Hitler made it unlikely that the president would support the man.

At this point, yet another schemer intervened—Joachim von Ribbentrop, a wealthy businessman and Nazi party member who had helped arrange Papen's discreet meetings with Hitler. Ribbentrop suggested bringing Oskar von Hindenburg into the intrigue; perhaps the father could be won over through his son. The younger Hindenburg was to be approached secretly, and Ribbentrop offered his home in a Berlin suburb for the encounter.

The security precautions on the evening of January 22 were elaborate. Oskar von Hindenburg and State Secretary Otto Meissner first appeared at the Berlin opera house for a performance of Wagner's *Das Liebesverbot*. At the intermission, Hindenburg, having been joined by his wife, made their presence conspicuous by greeting a large number of acquaintances. But as the houselights dimmed for the final act, Meissner and Hindenburg slipped out and hailed a taxi. To conceal their destination, they alighted before reaching Ribbentrop's home and tramped the last snowy stretch on foot.

Papen, Hitler, and others involved in the plot were waiting. The group conversed stiffly in the salon; then Hindenburg and Hitler closed themselves in an adjoining room, where they remained for more than an hour. No notes were taken, and only the two men were present, but Hitler, unable to persuade the older Hindenburg, was able to sway the younger. Later that evening, Oskar von Hindenburg confided to Meissner that he felt Hitler's entry into the government was inevitable.

A week of even more intense maneuvering began. Meeting followed meeting, and the ground underfoot grew ever more treacherous. Schleicher, his chancellorship threatened, had done little to help himself; his record of connivance and duplicity had alienated every faction in the Reichstag and, finally, President Hindenburg as well. Schleicher's dismissal appeared imminent. But Hindenburg, perhaps addled, assured those who called on him that he would appoint Papen—not Hitler—to the post. Papen, however, had begun to speak Hitler's name in the president's ear, quite loudly and insistently. The army's most important officers, too, had thrown their weight behind Hitler. Even Hindenburg's neighbor and close friend, the archconservative Count Elard von Oldenburg-Januschau, told the field marshal that he saw nothing to fear in appointing Hitler chancellor. There would be no trouble handling these young people, he said confidently; they were, after all, "quite attractive."

On January 28, the president faced his son Oskar, Otto Meissner, and Franz von Papen—the men in government he trusted most. They informed him bluntly that the only realistic course of action was to hand the government over to Hitler. In fact, Hitler, like the winds of a tornado, had created a political vacuum that only he could fill.

That same day, Schleicher was dismissed. The next morning, Hindenburg named Hitler, the man he had deemed too trivial to ever lead the country, to the post of Reich chancellor. Hitler pledged to observe the constitution and uphold the rights of the president. Above all, he said, he would knit together the fractured nation.

Throughout Germany, citizens marked the event. All day, crowds hailed the Führer—crowds far larger and more fervent than the small gathering that had watched Hitler drive to his first meeting with Hindenburg in October 1931. That night, the SA paraded in the streets by torchlight. Radio Cologne broadcast a message written by Nazi propagandists: "Like a blazing fire, the news spreads across Germany; Adolf Hitler is chancellor of the Reich! A million hearts are aflame. Rejoicing and gratitude pour forth."

In Detmold, capital of Lippe, where the Nazis had won their seminal victory two weeks earlier, a doctor spent the evening at the local hospital, tending the injured communists, socialists, and Jewish shopkeepers who had been beaten by the jubilant Brownshirts. And in Düsseldorf, where Hitler had spoken to the Industry Club, a threatening message was delivered to a communist sculptor who had hung a Red flag in his window. In the note were instructions that would enable him to flee to Holland by midnight if he valued his life.

In Berlin, as the night wore on, crowds passed along Wilhelmstrasse beneath the long narrow windows of the Reich Chancellery. From time to time, Hitler's nervous gesturing figure would appear in one of the windows. Farther along the facade, in another window, President Hindenburg stared out at the marching formations and absently tapped his cane to the beat of the martial music. The people in the street offered courteous homage to the old soldier. But their cheers for the new leader were ecstatic.

Despite Hitler's lofty promises, he had offered no new policies for governing, nor had he presented any new programs. Papen, the mainstay of the conspiracy to install Hitler, spoke for many who saw no need for such details. Hitler could be controlled. "In two months," Papen told a friend, "we'll have him backed into a corner so hard he'll be squeaking."

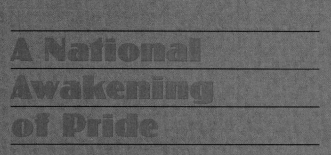

A National Awakening of Pride

The many celebrations staged across Germany to salute the National Socialists' accession to power in 1933 reached a still-broader audience with the publication of half a million copies of a lavishly illustrated book, *Deutschland Erwacht* (Germany awakens). Subtitled "Origins, Struggle, and Victory of the NSDAP," the book honored what its text described as the "heroics and courage of those who fought with unshaken confidence in a world of enemies."

Published by the Nazis in collaboration with a major cigarette manufacturer, *Deutschland Erwacht* was financed by a cleverly executed combination of marketing and propaganda. Copies of the book were distributed with pages containing blank spaces interspersed among the black-and-white illustrations. Brightly hand-colored photographs of Adolf Hitler and the rallies and other Nazi party functions were then inserted as premiums in packs of cigarettes. After removing these so-called cigarette cards, the buyer was to paste them into the designated white spaces in the volume.

A diligent collector could accumulate a series of unabashedly patriotic books in this way. Each volume chronicled the National Socialists' rise to power in an era when the art of photography was just emerging as an important instrument for reaching—and influencing—a massive audience. And few other events were better suited to the camera than the grand pageants at the ancient Bavarian city of Nuremberg and elsewhere *(shown on following pages)* that were glorified in *Deutschland Erwacht*.

The camera presents a Führer's-
eye view as Hitler prepares to
address an SA rally in the city of
Dortmund in July 1933. The book
Deutschland Erwacht lauded the
Brownshirts as "fighters sea-
soned in a thousand battles
on behalf of Adolf Hitler's ideas."

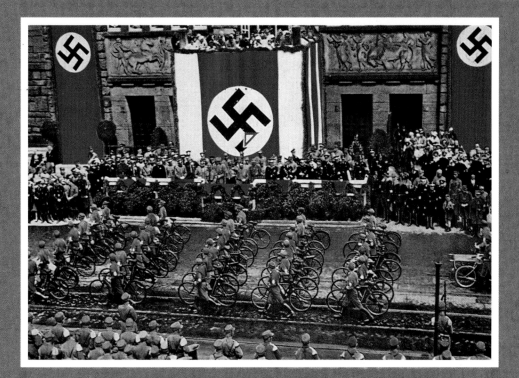

Brown-shirted members of the
SA Bicycle Corps pass in review
before Hitler and his entourage
during the Dortmund rally.

A smiling Joseph Goebbels (right)
joins other Nazi dignitaries in
saluting participants in the 1933
Stuttgart Gymnastics Festival.

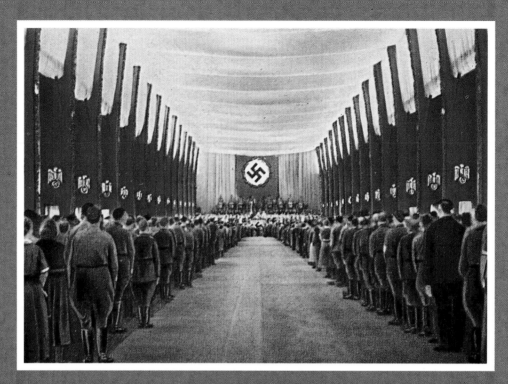

SA men stand at attention in
Nuremberg's Congress Hall,
where Rudolf Hess proclaimed
the 1933 convention open: "We
salute the Führer and, through
him, the future of our nation."

More than 100,000 members of
the SA and the SS assemble near
Nuremberg in what the book
Deutschland Erwacht called a
"symbol of the everlastingness
of National Socialist Germany."

Flag-carrying SA officers sweep in unison down the steps of the Luitpold Arena during a ceremonial roll call of Nazi party leaders at the 1933 Nuremberg rally.

Helmeted SS standard-bearers file into position on the Zeppelin Field, a broad meadow on the outskirts of Nuremberg, where the largest spectacles were held.

SA members marching in ranks
give the Nazi salute as they pass
the Führer during a parade
through the streets of Nuremberg's old quarter, which dates
back to the fourteenth century.

Spectators crowd into a massive
grandstand erected in front
of the Frauenkirche in Nuremberg's market square, which
was renamed Adolf Hitler Plaza.

In the final hours of the 1933
rally, a brigade of the Hitler
Youth is reviewed by its commander, Baldur von Schirach,
who salutes it from the Führer's
black Mercedes touring car.

"Now We Will Show Them!"

wo days after he swore in Adolf Hitler as chancellor, President Hindenburg received a telegram from an old comrade. The message came from General Erich Ludendorff, who not only had been Hindenburg's principal deputy during World War I but had also marched alongside Hitler in the Beer Hall Putsch of 1923. Instead of congratulating the president on his choice, Ludendorff expressed deep foreboding.

"By appointing Hitler chancellor of the Reich, you have handed over our sacred German fatherland to one of the greatest demagogues of all time," Ludendorff wrote. "I prophesy to you that this evil man will plunge our Reich into the abyss and will inflict immeasurable woe on our nation. Future generations will curse you in your grave." Hindenburg ignored the telegram, which he considered the ranting of an unstable mind. Sadly, the brilliant Ludendorff had fallen from his pinnacle as one of Germany's most distinguished soldiers. He had recently devised a pagan religion to go with his political radicalism, and even the Nazis disavowed him as deranged.

In any event, Hindenburg was confident that he and his conservative colleagues had a firm rein on Hitler. The new cabinet Hitler had to work with included only two other Nazis—Minister of the Interior Wilhelm Frick and Reichstag President Hermann Göring, who served without portfolio. The eight other members—soon to become nine with the appointment of a minister of justice—were either members of the Nationalist party or unaffiliated conservatives. Hindenburg had chosen them largely on the advice of his aristocratic friend, Franz von Papen, the former chancellor, who was expected to exert a calming influence on Hitler. Papen remained in the cabinet as vice chancellor and held other important cards as well. As Reich commissioner of Prussia, he controlled the administrative machinery of Germany's largest and most influential state. In addition, Hindenburg had promised never to meet with Hitler unless Papen was present. Papen insisted on this assurance because he feared that in a one-on-one encounter with the Nazi leader, the president, beset by periods of senility, might be talked into approving something that Papen disagreed with. If he were present, Papen thought, he could counter Hitler's arguments.

The wily Hitler understood Papen's game, and he was ready. "The reactionaries think they have put me on a leash," he remarked to a Nazi colleague. "They are going to set traps for me, as many as they can. But we will not wait until they act. We are ruthless. I have no bourgeois scruples! They think I am uncultured, a barbarian. Yes, we are barbarians! We want to be. That is an honorable title."

After only two days in office, Hitler had already outwitted Papen and his cabinet cronies and taken the first giant step on the path to dictatorship and the fulfillment of Ludendorff's prophecy. In a matter of months, Hitler's tactics of guile and intimidation, opportunism and terror—abetted by sheer good luck—would crush the power of the old guard and carry the former Austrian vagrant to absolute mastery over his adopted Reich.

Hitler's opening gambit was to maneuver the government into holding new elections. He saw immediately that such elections, in addition to lending him an aura of democratic legitimacy, could free him from the restraints that were imposed both by his conservative partners in the coalition government and by the German constitution. Now that the National Socialists could call upon government resources, Hitler was sure he could win enough seats in the Reichstag to render the coalition unnecessary. And if the Nazis could command two-thirds of the legislature, he could ram through so-called enabling legislation, suspending the constitution and allowing him to rule practically by fiat.

At a baser level, the Nazi-Nationalist coalition had to find forty-five additional seats just to attain the majority necessary to remain in power. Hitler made a pretense of trying to gain the support of the Catholic Center party's seventy deputies by negotiating with the party's leaders. These talks, however, were mere window dressing for the benefit of Papen and his Nationalist ally in the cabinet, Alfred Hugenberg, who opposed new elections. Hitler made certain that the talks would fail. On January 31, 1933, his first full day in office, he told the cabinet there was no hope of obtaining the Center party's backing. Without a majority, Hugenberg and Papen thus had no choice but to call upon Hindenburg to dissolve the Reichstag and announce new elections, which were scheduled for March 5.

Joseph Goebbels, the Nazi propaganda chief, sat down with his Führer and mapped out the party's most extensive election campaign ever. "The struggle is a light one now, since we are able to employ all the means of the state," Goebbels noted gleefully in his diary. "Radio and press are at our disposal. We shall achieve a masterpiece of propaganda."

Hitler took advantage of his new position by making a radio broadcast to the nation on February 1. His first speech as chancellor showed restraint

Ganz Deutschland hört den Führer

mit dem Volksempfänger

characteristic of a statesman. The Führer portrayed nazism as a unified national uprising against the evils of the Weimar Republic and pledged that the new government would "revive in the nation the spirit of unity and cooperation." Hitler also promised to promote Christianity "as the foundation of our national morality" and appealed for God's blessing on the work of his government.

Beyond these pieties, Hitler had few specific programs to offer. As he crisscrossed Germany by plane in the ensuing weeks, he repeated his basic theme. The message, as Hitler described it to members of the cabinet, his chest swelling with emotion, was simply, "Attack Marxism!" The Communists and Social Democrats were the undifferentiated targets, and Goebbels ensured that the Nazi campaign—as it resounded from home radios and from loudspeakers that were set up in streets and public squares—echoed with religious fervor. In some towns, pealing church bells introduced Nazi rallies, and Hitler solemnly concluded his most passionate speeches with a pious amen.

In addition to drawing on government resources, the Nazis tapped the financial assets of big business. On February 20, Göring invited a score of Germany's most powerful industrialists to his official residence in the palace next to the Reichstag building. The guests heard Hitler vow that this would be the last election and then add ominously, "If the election does not decide, the decision must be brought about by other means." When the hat was passed, the assembled moguls pledged the equivalent of one million dollars to the campaign. Most gave out of self-interest rather than from genuine sympathy for the Nazis. But the evening produced one notable convert. Gustav Krupp, who had previously shown little enthusiasm for Hitler, put up one-third of the total. Eventually, he would throw the support of the entire Krupp steel and armaments empire behind the new regime.

Hitler boosted the campaign further by exploiting the legislative powers of the government. In his first days in office, he pushed through the cabinet the so-called Decree for the Protection of the German People. Far from being protective, the order actually curtailed two basic freedoms—assembly and speech. It authorized the interior minister and the police to ban meetings deemed dangerous to public security, and to suppress any news-

paper, magazine, or book "whose contents are calculated to endanger public security or good order."

Although the measure contravened the spirit of the constitution and was clearly a ploy to curtail rival political parties, it was technically legal. The president could give such decrees the force of law under the emergency powers granted him by article 48 of the constitution. Papen and his right-wing friends were happy to prevail upon Hindenburg to sign the decree, since they saw it as aimed only at the hated Marxist Left. Despite protests from the political opposition, Hindenburg did not hesitate to approve this and a subsequent decree that dissolved the Prussian state legislature.

Göring's position in Prussia, where the former flying ace was minister of the interior, was probably the most effective instrument of government the Nazis enjoyed at the moment. Working day and night, he ignored his

Above, members of the Berlin police force, taken over by the Nazis, parade past their new partners in law enforcement, the SS. Inset, two SS men wear white bands to signify their deputization as auxiliary policemen.

nominal superior, Papen, and took control of Prussia's 90,000-man police organization, which served the capital, Berlin, and fully two-thirds of Germany's 60 million people. Göring quickly established harsh ground rules for the election campaign in Prussia. He banned meetings and demonstrations by the Communist party and suppressed the publication of opposition newspapers. At the same time, he began "cleaning out the Augean stables," as Goebbels put it, ruthlessly dumping hundreds of police officials and replacing them with Nazis.

Göring left no doubt as to how the Prussian police should conduct themselves. He ordered them to maintain the best relations with the Storm Troopers and the Stahlhelm but to show no mercy in suppressing the activities of subversive organizations—meaning the Communists and anyone else who dared to oppose the Nazis. He urged his men to use their firearms. Failure to shoot, he said, would be punished. And just in case his police did not get the message or were squeamish, Göring told them a few days later: "I must hammer it into your heads that the responsibility is mine alone. If you shoot, I also shoot. If someone lies dead there, I have shot him, even though I am sitting upstairs in the ministry building."

The line between law enforcement and terror was further blurred on February 22, when Göring deputized a new 50,000-man auxiliary police force on the pretext that Prussia's existing law-enforcement manpower was inadequate to preserve order. Most of the new men came from the SA and the SS. By simply affixing a white armband to their brown or black shirts, the Nazi toughs could now intimidate political opponents and personal enemies with official impunity.

As a result of Nazi violence—official and freelance—Prussia accounted for many of the fifty-one Nazi opponents murdered during the campaign. (The National Socialists reported losing eighteen lives from their own ranks.) Nor did other states escape the bloodletting. A prominent politician in Württemberg protested to Hindenburg that Storm Trooper assaults on party rallies there threatened to turn the campaign into "open civil war."

Hitler's strategy of legal revolution required the use of subtler tactics than open warfare. The Nazis wanted to provoke the communists into acts of violence; the government could then crack down and crush them under the cloak of legality. "For the present, we shall abstain from direct action,"

Goebbels noted in his diary. "First, the bolshevist attempt at a revolution must burst into flame. At the given moment, we shall strike."

The problem, however, was that three weeks into the campaign, the Red menace had failed to materialize. The Communists, who had made their best showing ever in the previous election, drawing nearly six million votes, were now practically invisible. They lay low in the mistaken belief that Hitler was merely the puppet of reactionaries whose policies would inevitably bring on the collapse of the capitalist system. Then, less than a week before the election, came a stunning event that seemed to fulfill Goebbels's requirement for a bolshevist outburst.

The torchbearer was a twenty-four-year-old Dutch itinerant named Marinus van der Lubbe. Half-blind, demented-looking, shabbily dressed in a peaked cap and trousers too short for him, van der Lubbe was the image of a political revolutionary. He had come by this calling the hard way. The son of a street peddler who had abandoned the family and a mother who had died when he was twelve, Marinus had been apprenticed to a bricklayer and suffered damage to both eyes in accidents involving caustic lime. Originally a Calvinist, he converted to communism. He wrote pamphlets attacking capitalism, spoke at meetings, and led demonstrations. But he was a maverick by nature, and in 1931 he broke with his orthodox comrades and joined a splinter group of Dutch anarchists known as the Party of International Communists, who were opposed to Moscow.

Attracted by the election campaign in neighboring Germany, van der Lubbe traveled there from his native Leiden in February of 1933. Despite suffering both from asthma and from infections in his damaged eyes, he walked most of the 400 miles to the city of Berlin. There he found the Communists and other leftists so apathetic that he decided only drastic action could rouse them to revolt. On February 25, he purchased several packages of firestarters—a mixture of sawdust and naphthalene used to touch off coal fires—and set out to ignite the revolution. He lighted fires in three public buildings that day: the welfare office in suburban Neukölln, the Schöneberg town hall, and the old imperial palace. All three blazes were quickly discovered and doused.

The following day, van der Lubbe walked to a town outside Berlin and, as required by law, registered with the police as an alien. The police pitied the Dutch vagrant and allowed him to spend that night in a small cell. On the morning of February 27, van der Lubbe decided to attack a better-known building, one symbolic of Germany's political system. He headed through the cold for the center of Berlin to reconnoiter the next target of his political pyromania: the ornate, gilded, and glass-domed structure that housed the national parliament.

Dutch communist Marinus van der Lubbe holds the incendiary material he used to set fire to the Reichstag, shown burning in the background. Van der Lubbe "panted as if he had completed a tremendous task," reported one of the policemen who arrested him. "There was a triumphant gleam in the burning eyes of his pale, haggard, young face."

Van der Lubbe studied the Reichstag that afternoon and returned about nine o'clock in the evening with a fresh supply of firestarters in his pockets. He went to the unlit western side of the building, which was deserted, and scrambled up the wall to a first-floor balcony at the front of the Reichstag's restaurant. Van der Lubbe kicked in the thick window panes, jumped through, and started work.

The intruder ran from room to room in the enormous building, touching off small blazes. After he had exhausted his four packages of firestarters, he improvised torches from anything he could lay his hands on: a table-cloth, towels, even his own shirt, waistcoat, and overcoat, which he had stripped off because of the stifling heat. Reaching the cavernous Sessions

Chamber where the deputies met, he ripped down some musty draperies and ignited them. He dragged the burning drapes behind him and used them to set fire to others. Soon, columns of flame were climbing the tinder-dry wooden paneling on the walls.

Suddenly van der Lubbe heard approaching voices. He dashed through a hallway into Bismarck Hall, a large room at the rear of the building, and found the exit door locked. He turned and ran back—into the arms of two police officers. It was 9:27, and at that moment an explosion, caused by an accumulation of gases from the fire, ripped through the overarching glass dome of the Sessions Chamber.

The Dutchman surrendered without a struggle. Naked to the waist and with a mat of tangled hair clinging to his sweat-smeared face, he was hustled off to a building entrance. A policeman noticed him shivering in the cold and threw a rug over his bare back. While firefighters rushed in to battle the blaze, van der Lubbe was taken to the nearby Brandenburg Gate station. There, speaking in heavily accented but fluent German, he readily confessed to setting the fire and said he had acted alone.

Hitler was relaxing after dinner at ten o'clock that evening in Goebbels's Berlin apartment when the phone rang. The caller was Ernst Hanfstaengl, the Harvard-educated Nazi foreign press chief and a notorious practical joker. When told the news, Goebbels at first thought Hanfstaengl was playing a prank and refused to inform Hitler. But Goebbels soon confirmed the report, and he and the Führer sped to the scene in the chancellor's large Mercedes touring car.

At the Reichstag, which was now ringed by sixty fire engines, Goebbels and Hitler were greeted by Göring, who had rushed over from the Prussian Interior Ministry in the hope of saving the family tapestries that hung in his Reichstag office. Göring had learned of van der Lubbe's arrest, heard that a pair of Communist members of the Reichstag had left the building only about twenty minutes before the fire, and quickly concluded—as he exclaimed to a subordinate—"This is the beginning of the communist revolt!" He assured the Führer that he had mobilized the police and posted guards at every public building in Berlin.

Hitler wanted to believe that the moment he had dreamed of was here at last: The communist revolution had begun, and now he could save Germany. Excitedly, he toured the still-burning building and met Papen, who had been attending a dinner in honor of President Hindenburg at the nearby Herrenklub. Hitler shook Papen's hand vigorously and cried out, "This is a God-given signal, Herr Vice Chancellor."

A few minutes later, Hitler stood on a balcony overlooking the Sessions Chamber, where the heat had been so intense it had twisted the iron pillars.

Police and fire officials inspect the Reichstag's burned-out Sessions Chamber on the morning following the fire. The gutted meeting hall would not be restored until 1971.

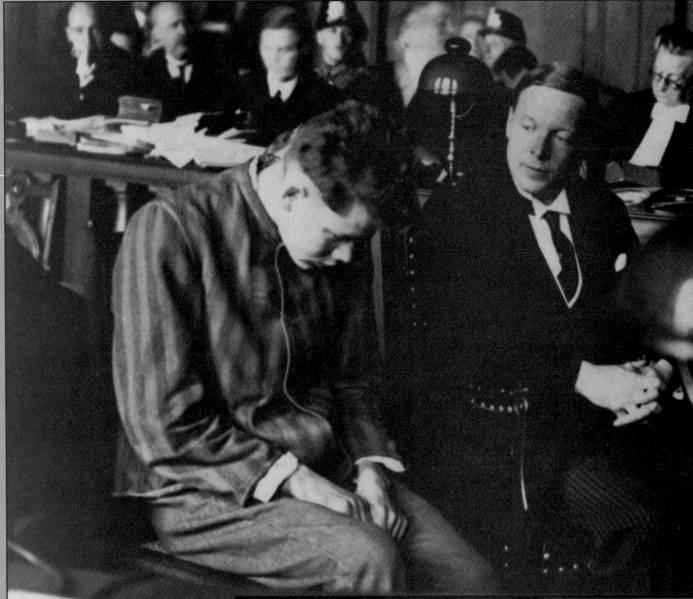

Van der Lubbe—the only defendant required to wear shackles
and a prison uniform—is questioned by his court-appointed
translator. The young revolutionary's health and morale
deteriorated during the trial.

Hermann Göring confronts the
defendant Georgi Dimitrov
(*standing, facing him*). Rebuked by
the judge for spouting communist propaganda, Dimitrov attacked Göring: "But he is making
National Socialist propaganda!"

The defendants' families nervously await the verdict. Though acquitted, Torgler was held in prison two more years; the Bulgarians were sent to Moscow in exchange for some alleged German agents.

A Trial That Backfired

When the Reichstag-fire trial began on September 21, 1933, the guilt of Marinus van der Lubbe, the Dutch arsonist caught red-handed at the scene, was not in doubt. The question that fascinated the world was: Whom was he working for?

The Nazis claimed that van der Lubbe was in league with the four communists beside him in the dock: Ernst Torgler, the leader of the German Communist party, and Bulgarians Georgi Dimitrov, Vassili Tanev, and Blagoi Popov. The communists in turn accused the Nazis of orchestrating the fire and mounted a worldwide propaganda campaign intended to portray van der Lubbe as a stooge of the Nazis.

Dimitrov—who, unbeknown to the Nazis, was a senior official of the Communist International—turned the tables on the prosecution with his razor-sharp wit. Acting as his own attorney, he ridiculed the 235-page-long indictment as remarkable only because of its length. He described van der Lubbe as a "miserable Faust" controlled by an unidentified Nazi Mephistopheles.

When the prosecution could not locate a certain witness, Dimitrov asked caustically, "Have you looked for him in a concentration camp?" The high point of the trial was Dimitrov's cross-examination of Hermann Göring (*left*), president of the Reichstag; the needling interrogation ended with Göring shouting in rage, "Wait till I get you outside the power of this court!"

After fifty-seven days of what a foreign journalist called "superlative drama," only van der Lubbe, who insisted all along that he had acted alone, was found guilty. On January 10, 1934, he was beheaded.

Leaning over the stony parapet, he stared down into the dying flames, pondering the conflagration that seemed sent from heaven. Suddenly, his face flushed with heat and emotion, he turned to his companions and shouted: "Now we will show them! Anyone in our path will be mowed down! The German people have been been soft too long! Every Communist official must be shot! All Communist sympathizers must be locked up! And that goes for the Social Democrats, too!"

While Hitler and Goebbels stopped the presses and remade the front page of the Nazi daily newspaper *Völkischer Beobachter*, Göring, the man of many hats, tended to several tasks. He rewrote the first report from the official press service so that it left no doubt the fire "was intended to be the signal for a bloody uprising and civil war." He immediately prohibited all Communist publications in Prussia for four months and all Social Democratic publications for two weeks. Göring also sent the police and Storm Troopers into the night armed with a list of 4,000 Communist functionaries; the names had been compiled by his Social Democratic predecessor. Before morning, hundreds of people whose names were on the list—and scores of others the National Socialists simply did not like—were

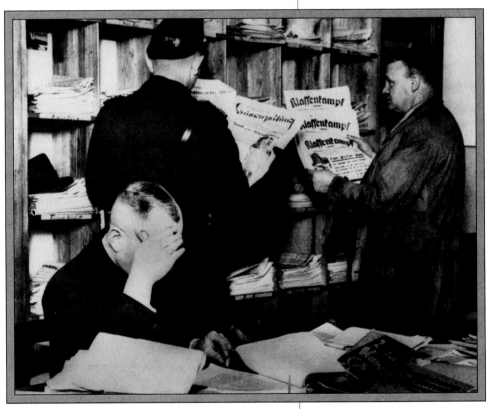

Police study leaflets entitled *Klassenkampf* (Class struggle) seized at Communist headquarters three days before the Reichstag fire. The government promised to justify the raid by airing evidence of a revolutionary Red plot—but never did.

dragged from their beds at gunpoint and beaten, shot, drowned, or jailed.

The day after the fire, February 28, Hitler moved to legalize this reign of terror. Under the pretext of warding off a Red uprising, he proposed an emergency decree that suspended more fundamental liberties than any earlier act: It empowered the police to monitor private telephone calls and intercept mail and telegrams. An individual's right to legal counsel was denied, and an accused person could be imprisoned without a hearing or trial. The decree authorized the federal government to assume control of any state that was unable to maintain order, and it made arson, sabotage, and other crimes supposedly planned by communist conspirators punishable by death. Fear of the Red menace was so acute that the cabinet quickly approved the suspension of civil liberties—only the provision about taking over state governments occasioned any debate—and Hindenburg signed the decree into law that evening without so much as a comment. All power now lay in the hands of the central government.

The communist conspiracy behind the Reichstag fire proved nonexistent. The government eventually brought to trial a quartet of defendants in addition to van der Lubbe *(pages 154-155)*. One of them was Ernst Torgler, leader of the Communist faction in the Reichstag. The three others were Bulgarians who turned out to be agents of Moscow but had nothing to do with the fire. To the embarrassment of the Nazis, the court acquitted everyone except van der Lubbe, who was executed in January 1934, still claiming he had acted alone.

Because the fire had been a godsend for Hitler, an entirely different conspiracy theory took root. According to this notion, which was assiduously promoted by the communists and widely believed outside of Germany, the Nazis had staged the whole affair and made a dupe of the young Dutchman. Heat pipes ran through an underground passage between the Reichstag and Göring's nearby official residence. Supposedly, a team of Storm Troopers had sneaked through the tunnel and spread incendiary chemicals just before van der Lubbe arrived. An international campaign that was skillfully masterminded by Willi Münzenberg, an expatriate German communist, nurtured the myth. In fact, however, no convincing evidence was ever brought forth to demonstrate that anyone other than van der Lubbe caused the fire.

What mattered in 1933, in the few remaining days before the March 5 election, was not the origin but the German perception of the Reichstag fire. The National Socialists played upon public anxiety with harrowing accounts of purported Red plots to kidnap, burn, poison, and assassinate. The lurid plans were allegedly detailed in documents discovered during a raid on Communist party headquarters in Berlin three days before the fire. Although not a shred of evidence was made public, many Germans swallowed the story word for word.

At the same time, the emergency decree occasioned by the fire provided Hitler with a perversely legal foundation for terror and intimidation. The Nazi-run government was now free to hound the opposition, to suppress, search, confiscate, arrest, and detain at will. In Göring's Prussia alone, an estimated 10,000 people were arrested in the two weeks after approval of the decree on February 28. When jails and prisons overflowed, the first Nazi concentration camps were authorized. No longer did Göring have to gloss over his brutal concept of public service, which he made brazenly clear to an audience in Frankfurt on March 3. "My business is not to dispense justice," he said, "but to destroy and exterminate."

The political campaign reached its frenzied climax on the following day, Saturday, March 4, the eve of the election. At the end of this "Day of National Awakening," which Goebbels had named and orchestrated, Hitler delivered a speech that was broadcast nationwide on radio from Königsberg, formerly the site of imperial coronations. When the Führer had finished exhorting German listeners to "hold your heads high and proudly once more," the bells of local cathedrals rang out, bonfires--Goebbels called them "fires of freedom"--blazed on lofty mountaintops all over the Reich, and, in the streets of every city and town, the boots of marching Storm Troopers beat a menacing tattoo.

The Nazi hoopla produced a huge voter turnout. Nearly nine of ten eligible Germans voted. It was to be the last honestly counted election held under Hitler's auspices, and despite the cacophony of propaganda and intimidation, the National Socialists received only 44 percent of the vote. Yet this was a substantial improvement over their 33-percent pull in the previous election, and Nazi representation in the Reichstag increased from 196 to 288 seats. In order to achieve a majority, Hitler still needed the coalition with the Nationalists, who again won 52 seats with 8 percent of the vote. The left-wing targets of the Nazi campaign fared better than expected: The Communists lost 19 of their 100 seats; the Social Democrats, only one of their 121 seats.

Undeterred by the modest results, Hitler claimed a victory so overwhelming that it constituted a revolution, and he accelerated his drive for absolute power. His first step was to initiate *Gleichschaltung*, or coordination, a euphemism for the process of forcibly bringing under control of the Nazi party the political, economic, and social life of the nation.

The term *Gleichschaltung* was first applied to the nazification of federal states. Governed by their own parliaments, they had stubbornly maintained separate powers throughout German history. Now Hitler began stamping out the system of state self-government. In Bavaria, where there had been talk of restoration of the monarchy and even of secession, the Nazis turned out the elected government on March 9 with a show of force and installed a special commissioner appointed by Hitler. Similarly, in a number of other states, Storm Troopers acting on instructions from Berlin stirred up sufficient trouble to give the national government excuses to intervene and appoint Nazi officials to keep order. By March 15, all of Germany's seventeen states were under Nazi control.

Members of the Stahlhelm, the veterans' arm of the Nationalist party, wave the imperial colors as they pass the Brandenburg Gate. The Nationalists won fifty-two seats in March 1933, enough for a Nazi-Nationalist majority in the Reichstag.

Next, Hitler intended to induce members of the Reichstag to gut their own legislative powers as thoroughly as flames had destroyed the Reichstag chamber. First, however, he needed to strengthen his position with the generals, the conservatives, and others who felt strong ties to the old imperial traditions. He accomplished this by staging a magnificent opening ceremony for the new session of the Reichstag at the tradition-steeped town of Potsdam. Once the residence of Prussia's kings, the city had come to symbolize Prussian militarism.

The ceremony was planned and directed by Goebbels, who had filled the new post of minister of public enlightenment and propaganda on March 13. With his uncanny instinct for theater, Goebbels set about creating the illusion of a reconciliation between the old Germany and the new. The site, the Garrison Church, stood atop the tomb of Frederick the Great, the eighteenth-century king of Prussia. The date, March 21, heralded not only the beginning of spring but also the anniversary of the historic day in 1871 when Bismarck opened the first Reichstag of the German empire. And the trappings artfully blended the symbols of tradition and nazism. The guard of honor consisted of gray-clad members of the Reichswehr drawn up on one side and brown-shirted Storm Troopers on the other. The swastika and the old black, white, and red imperial flag flew side by side. They had recently been decreed the official banners of Germany, replacing the black, red, and gold of the Weimar Republic.

The ceremonies went forward according to script. Aged generals and admirals from the imperial days turned one entire gallery into a sea of gold-braided and bemedaled uniforms. A chair had even been reserved for the exiled kaiser; as Hindenburg, resplendent in his field marshal's dress uniform, shuffled slowly to his seat of honor, he bowed and raised his baton in salute to the kaiser's empty throne.

Hitler played the dutiful acolyte. Looking ill at ease in a cutaway coat —"like a timid newcomer being introduced by an important protector into company to which he does not belong," observed the French ambassador—Hitler paid extravagant homage to Hindenburg: "We consider it a blessing to have your consent to the German rising." Then, in a shrewd gesture that symbolically linked the Nazi party to the glories of the Prussian past, Hitler walked over to Hindenburg's chair and bent low to grasp his hand. Tears in his eyes, the old soldier rose and placed a wreath upon the tomb of Frederick the Great while cannons boomed outside.

By his performance at Potsdam, Hitler convinced many of those who had voted against him that his intentions were honorable. He next turned his energies to freeing himself from the constitutional constraints imposed on him by the office of president and the Reichstag. His instrument was the

Enabling Act, formally known as the Law for the Removal of the Distress of People and Reich. If enacted, the measure would enable Hitler as chancellor to promulgate domestic laws and foreign treaties for the next four years. He could do this without parliamentary approval, without adhering to the constitution, and without the involvement of the president, who until now possessed the sole power to issue emergency decrees independent of the Reichstag.

Far from being pushed into a corner by the conservatives, as Papen had predicted, Hitler had so tamed his coalition partners that he could propose to make himself dictator. Papen and the cabinet, still in the combined grip of the Red scare and the nationalistic euphoria of Potsdam, voiced no serious objections. As for the aged president, the guardian of the constitution, he was reportedly pleased to be relieved of the burden of issuing unpopular emergency decrees.

On March 23, two days after the ceremonial opening at Potsdam, Hitler laid the proposal before the first working session of the Reichstag. The deputies, making their way into temporary quarters at Berlin's Kroll Opera House, had had to pass through menacing rows of Storm Troopers and black-shirted SS guards. In a restrained speech, Hitler proclaimed war on unemployment and promised to respect the rights of the states, churches, and private property. He said he would wield the powers of the Enabling Act "only insofar as they are essential for carrying out vitally necessary measures." Near the end, however, Hitler changed his tone, implying that he would push ahead with the law even if the Reichstag refused to approve it. He challenged the deputies to cooperate or suffer the consequences— "to decide between war and peace."

Passage of the Enabling Act required a two-thirds majority. Hitler did not have to worry about the votes of the eighty-one Communist deputies, who were either in jail or on the run. If he desired, Hitler could have eliminated the expected negative votes of the Social Democrats, too, by invoking the emergency decree of February 28 to jail these opposition deputies. But Hitler wanted to preserve the veneer of legality. In order to win the necessary votes, he had been courting the deputies of the Catholic Center party with a litany of dubious promises, including the assurance that no law would be promulgated without the president's approval. These pledges became the subject of a bitter debate during the Center party caucus that immediately followed Hitler's speech. The opposition was led by the former chancellor Heinrich Brüning, who called Hitler's proposal the "most monstrous thing ever demanded of a parliament."

When the Reichstag reconvened after a three-hour recess, a single deputy summoned the courage to speak against the Enabling Act. He was Otto

Wels, the leader of the Social Democrats, an upholsterer by profession and a member of the Reichstag since 1912. Wels was one of 94 Social Democratic deputies present on that historic day—the others in the party's 120-member delegation were in custody or were hiding from Nazi prosecution. He was not ordinarily much of an orator, and at first he was drowned out by the Storm Troopers drawn up outside the opera house who chanted, "We want the bill—or fire and murder!" But his voice gained in strength and eloquence. "Freedom and life can be taken away from us, but not our honor," he bravely declared. "No enabling act can give you the power to destroy ideas that are eternal and indestructible."

While Wels spoke to the Reichstag, Hitler prepared his reply. He had already seen a printed copy of the Social Democrat's address, which had been distributed to members of the press beforehand, and he hurriedly scribbled notes. As soon as Wels finished, Hitler sprang to his feet, brushed aside Papen, who tried to restrain him, and rushed to the rostrum. Pointing his finger directly at Wels, he delivered a savage rebuttal. "I do not want your votes. Germany will be free, but not through you," he shouted. "Do not mistake us for bourgeois. The star of Germany is in the ascendant! Yours is about to disappear! Your death knell has sounded!"

The balloting that ensued hinged upon the decision of the Catholic Center deputies, who had agreed to vote as a bloc. They were impressed by Hitler's promises to respect religion, and they feared that, if they opposed him, he might fire the many civil servants who belonged to the party and thus diminish the Center's influence on policy. The Center cast its votes in favor of the Enabling Act. In fact, the Center delegates and other non-Socialist members of the Reichstag proved so subservient—the final tally was 444 to 94—that Hitler could have gained his two-thirds majority even if the

Below, police struggle to restrain enthusiastic spectators at the opening of the first Nazi-led Reichstag in Potsdam. In the inset, Chancellor Hitler chats amiably with a representative of the old order, Crown Prince Wilhelm, son of the exiled kaiser.

Communist deputies had not been excluded. Only the Social Democratic representatives voted against the measure—and thus voted in favor of preserving parliamentary democracy.

The Enabling Act, together with the emergency decree of February 28, became the legal basis for Hitler's Third Reich. Armed with the virtually unlimited powers granted by these two laws, Hitler and his followers had in their hands the political machinery to nazify the nation. The Enabling Act allowed Hitler to continue his policy of coordination full-bore. He issued a series of decrees that progressively swept away all vestiges of state sovereignty. First he temporarily dissolved the state parliaments; then he appointed special governors—most of them Nazi gauleiters—to preside over the states. They were empowered to dismiss parliaments, hire and fire

Jews taken into custody in 1933 watch anxiously from a Berlin police van as their identification booklets are examined by plain-clothes Gestapo agents and an SS officer. Repression of the Jews began early in Hitler's regime, when they were banned from the government, the universities, and the professions.

government personnel, and otherwise carry out the political directions set forth by the Reich chancellor. In the pivotal state of Prussia, Hitler elbowed aside the nominal chief executive, Papen, made himself governor, and promptly delegated his powers to Göring, who in effect was already running things there in his high-handed manner. A decree that was issued later further reduced the state governments to "merely administrative bodies of the Reich," in the words of Interior Minister Frick, who became responsible for administering them.

Hitler singled out for coordination another venerable institution, the civil service, which employed 1.6 million Germans and was renowned for its integrity and political neutrality. His Civil Service Law of April 7 legalized the firing of any worker with leftist or even republican sympathies and purged the civil service of employees not of Aryan descent. The law was the first of more than 400 decrees that progressively excluded the nation's 500,000 Jews from participation in German life.

Hitler had taken a step against the Jews a week earlier, though with less effect. The rate of anti-Semitic violence by the Storm Troopers had stepped up since the Reichstag fire, and reports of beatings and murders had appeared in foreign newspapers. Goebbels and Julius Streicher, founder of the notoriously anti-Semitic newspaper *Der Stürmer*, had pushed Hitler to proclaim a one-day boycott of Jewish businesses for Saturday, April 1. But the boycott had been less than a success; surprising numbers of German shoppers had braved the brown-shirted pickets and patronized their favorite Jewish-owned stores. Goebbels, who never acknowledged such failures, was breathless at the rapid pace of developments. "In the cabinet, the Führer's authority carries all before it," he recorded in his diary on April 22. "There is no more voting. The Führer decides. Everything moves much faster than we dared hope."

Aside from trying to intimidate the Jews, Goebbels's special concern was the coordination of cultural life. Under his leadership, musicians, singers, and actors who were deemed Marxist, Jewish, or otherwise un-German were fired. Scientists and other intellectuals were harassed. Goebbels also sent gangs of Nazi youths into university libraries to cart out objectionable books and burn them. In Berlin on May 10, books by the carload were set afire in front of the Kroll Opera House, while a Storm Trooper band played patriotic songs and Goebbels praised this "strong, great, and symbolic act." Among the works consumed in the bonfires were those of the nineteenth-century German poet Heinrich Heine, who had once written, "Wherever they burn books, they will also, in the end, burn human beings."

Hitler, meanwhile, targeted for coordination one of Germany's most powerful institutions—the trade-union movement. German unions boasted a combined membership of nearly six million workers, and the movement was dominated by the Social Democrats. Hitler saw organized labor as a threat. Still vivid in his memory was the general strike mounted by the unions in 1920 in order to cripple the so-called Kapp Putsch, the right-wing cabal led by the journalist Wolfgang Kapp that had briefly seized control of the national government.

To break the unions, Hitler used the one-two-three punch so characteristic of his tactics: intimidation through random violence, followed first by friendly overtures and then by brutal pressure. In March and April, he ordered the SA to take over local union offices and harass the leaders. As a result, union leaders, out of desperation and fear, adopted a conciliatory stance toward the new chancellor. He in turn granted an old labor-union demand, making May 1—for decades a day of celebration for German workers—a paid national holiday. To celebrate the event, Goebbels organized one of his extravaganzas, complete with parade and mass rally. Union officials ordered the rank and file to participate, and that night more than one million white- and blue-collar workers marched under the swastika to Berlin's Tempelhof airfield to hear Hitler speak. The lights were turned out, and the vast audience listened in darkness while Hitler—bathed in floodlights—pronounced an end to class warfare and declared the day's motto, "Honor work, and respect the worker."

Early the next morning, the SA and the SS struck. They occupied union offices all over Germany, confiscated funds, and jailed labor leaders who only the day before had cooperated with Hitler in staging Germany's new May Day. Before the end of the month, Hitler effectively abolished collective bargaining by putting all matters concerning wages and working conditions in the hands of government-appointed labor trustees. All trade unions were dissolved and their members transferred to the German Labor Front, under the leadership of the longtime drunkard and Nazi gauleiter in Cologne, Robert Ley. Although Ley was a peasant's son and liked to talk of his lower-class origins, he promised "to restore absolute leadership to the natural leader of a factory—that is, the employer."

Having coordinated the states, the civil service, and labor, Hitler turned his attention to the political parties. The Communists had been outlawed for all practical purposes since the Reichstag fire, and this process was formally completed with confiscation of the party's assets. Next to feel the pressure were the Social Democrats; Göring had their offices and other properties seized on May 10. While some leaders stayed on and tried to appease the Nazis, the courageous chairman who had stood up to Hitler in the Reichstag, Otto Wels, fled to Prague and established the party in exile. He left behind an anti-Nazi underground that worried Hitler and caused

After raiding a union headquarters in Leipzig, Storm Troopers sift through the rubble. Hitler broke Germany's trade unions by arresting their leaders, confiscating union funds, and merging the rank and file into the Nazi-run Labor Front.

him to formally ban the Social Democrats on June 22 as "subversive and inimical to the state."

The middle-class parties took the hint. All of them disbanded less than a fortnight after the Socialists were banned—the State party, the German People's party, the Christian Socialist party, the Bavarian People's party, and finally, on July 5, the Catholic Center party. Notwithstanding its ti-

midity in the matter of the Enabling Act, the Center had served the nation and the Roman Catholic church for more than sixty years and had been a bulwark of the Weimar Republic. Its dissolution, however, did not deter the Vatican from negotiating a concordat with Germany under which the church agreed to keep priests out of politics and Hitler pledged freedom for the Catholic schools.

Most surprising of all was the swift collapse of Hitler's coalition partners, the Nationalists. No longer in need of their votes in the Reichstag—the Enabling Act had taken care of that—Hitler put pressure on the Nationalists' leader, Alfred Hugenberg. He treated Hugenberg with contempt in

In massive unison, 300,000 Germans give the Nazi salute during a demonstration in Berlin against the Versailles treaty in June 1933. Hitler's promise to abrogate the hated treaty became a rallying cry for the nation.

the cabinet and orchestrated demands for his resignation from farm groups and others. The police and Storm Troopers arrested Nationalists and terrorized their meetings and, on June 21, seized party offices all over Germany. Six days later, after Hugenberg's appeals to the president went unheeded, he submitted his resignation from the cabinet and, on the same day, disbanded the party.

All of this left Germany with a single political organization, the National Socialist German Workers' party. On July 14, a government decree made that official, declaring it a crime punishable by up to three years in prison to start a rival party. The political opposition had been eliminated with such breathtaking speed that Hitler himself could scarcely believe it. "One would never have thought so miserable a collapse possible," he remarked scornfully early in July.

The cabinet, too, was now coordinated. Two Nazis replaced Hugenberg in his twin posts as minister of economics and minister of food and agriculture. Rudolf Hess, Hitler's deputy in the Nazi party, started attending cabinet meetings, and the remaining non-Nazis in the cabinet converted, either in spirit or by actually joining the party. Papen, squeezed out of his commissioner's role in Prussia, was also losing influence nationally; at Hindenburg's request, he no longer sat in when Hitler and Hindenburg conferred. The president, ailing in mind and body, seemed thoroughly enchanted, if sometimes befuddled, by his dynamic new chancellor. He was so agreeable to what Hitler wanted and so eclipsed in power by Hitler's machinations that a friend referred to Hindenburg as the "president we no longer have." Nonetheless, the old war hero continued to elicit warm respect from the German people. He also maintained his constitutional title of commander in chief of the armed forces and took it seriously. One of the rare occasions when Hitler backed down was after Hindenburg had opposed his choice for commander of the German army.

For all his newly acquired power, Hitler could not become absolute master of Germany as long as the president clung to supreme command of the army. Throughout the autumn of 1933, Hitler concentrated on his short-term goal of putting unemployed Germans back to work and his long-term aim of rearmament and foreign expansion. He and Goebbels shrewdly showcased each new program with a display of propaganda and public involvement so vigorous that the entire nation appeared to be swept up in enthusiasm for the Nazi regime. This sleight of hand was particularly evident in Hitler's most enduring project, the construction of the autobahns. The 2,500-mile-long network of highways linking the major cities of the Reich was by far the largest public-works project launched during 1933.

Building the autobahns was the ideal government program: It created jobs, served both civilian and military needs, and satisfied Hitler's desire for "grand, monumental works to set the German economy in motion." At the groundbreaking ceremony on September 23 for the initial section of road between the cities of Frankfurt and Mannheim, the Führer himself turned the first shovels of earth—smiling knowledgeably, as if he were accustomed to performing manual labor.

The autobahn project was to prove so popular that the Nazi publicity machine soon lauded Hitler as the visionary who had conceived the idea. In fact, Hitler had opposed the project. Its chief longtime proponents belonged to an organization called Hafraba, which had been founded in 1926 to promote construction of a highway from Hamburg to Basel via Frankfurt. Four years later, when a majority in the Reichstag appeared to be on the brink of supporting Hafraba, Nazi deputies joined with the Communists to block the legislation. After construction began, however, the Nazi engineer in charge of the project, Fritz Todt, wrote Hafraba and warned its members against taking any credit. The autobahns, Todt wrote, were "solely and exclusively Adolf Hitler's roads."

Hitler also used his first major foray into foreign policy to solidify his domestic power base. In a radio broadcast on October 14, he announced that Germany was withdrawing from both the League of Nations and the Geneva Disarmament Conference. He blamed the move on an "intolerable humiliation"—the refusal of the other European powers to grant Germany full equality in armaments. Hitler was risking foreign sanctions, even a possible invasion. But by vowing to put the decision to the German people in a plebiscite, he knocked the democratic nations of the world off balance. After all, how could they object to a seemingly democratic process? He set the vote for November 12, the day after the anniversary of the World War I armistice, which for most Germans symbolized defeat and the dishonor imposed by the Versailles treaty.

Hitler campaigned hard for approval in the plebiscite. "See to it," he told a huge gathering in Breslau, "that this day shall be recorded in the history of our people as a day of salvation—that the record shall run, 'On an eleventh of November, the German people formally lost its honor; fifteen years later came a twelfth of November, and the German people restored honor to itself.'" New Reichstag elections were scheduled simultaneously, and Hitler even prevailed upon Hindenburg to address the nation in support of the government. The result of the election was a foregone conclusion, since voters were offered only the Nazi slate, which included Hugenberg and a score of guest candidates who had belonged to other parties before they were outlawed.

The outcome of both the election and the foreign-policy plebiscite was highly favorable. In both instances, more than 95 percent of all eligible voters cast ballots—not surprising since the Nazis had made voting mandatory. Of the valid ballots, 95.1 percent approved Hitler's repudiation of membership in the international community. In the Reichstag voting, the Nazis took control of all 639 seats. Intimidation and manipulation marked some of the balloting. For example, it was reported that 2,154 of the 2,242 inmates at the Dachau concentration camp near Munich voted for the government. But even without such dubious support, the overall numbers in Hitler's favor were so formidable as to constitute a clear mandate.

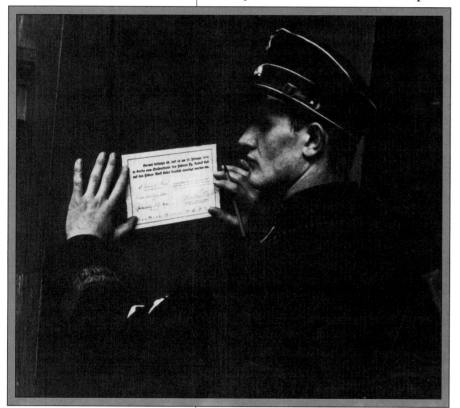

An SS man signs an oath confirming his allegiance to the Führer. The vow, which was printed on the card's reverse side, declared, "I swear unswerving loyalty to Adolf Hitler, absolute obedience to him and to the leaders appointed by him."

On January 30, 1934, the first anniversary of his appointment as chancellor, Hitler had every reason to count his blessings. His Nazis had seized control of Germany by largely legal means and with less bloodshed than anticipated. Thanks to public works and an expanding budget for army and armament, unemployment was down by nearly 40 percent. The process of breaking the shackles locked on at Versailles had begun. And despite all the National Socialists had done to destroy freedom in the new Reich, the president and an apparent majority of the people approved of Hitler's policies: On the anniversary, Hindenburg sent his chancellor "sincere appreciation for your devoted work and great achievements."

Even on this day of celebration, however, Hitler's first major crisis in office was taking shape. It arose not from opposition groups, all of whom had been crushed, but from disgruntled factions within the Nazi party. Discontent festered among the "old fighters," longtime members of the party who felt the Nazi revolution had not been carried far enough. Some were political radicals who took seriously the anticapitalist planks in the party's original program. Others were men from impoverished backgrounds who had looked forward to getting good jobs and sharing in the fruits of a Nazi regime. Instead, although Hitler had destroyed the communists and socialists on the left, he had compromised with the institutions on the right that traditionally ran Germany. Big business, the Junker landlords, the Prussian generals, even the civil service maintained much of their old power and influence.

The discontent swirled around the stocky figure of Ernst Röhm, chief of staff of the SA. Röhm was among Hitler's oldest colleagues, one of a handful of intimates with whom the Führer used the familiar form of address *du*. Röhm coined the slogan "second revolution" to refer to his goal of a far more radical transformation of German society. He had publicly attacked reactionaries, criticized the government, referred to Hitler in private as a swine, and stirred the pride of his Storm Troopers by calling them the incorruptible guarantors of the revolution. At the same time, he had shep-

SA men lead a parade in May 1933 in memory of Albert Schlageter, whom the French executed in 1923 for blowing up a bridge in the occupied Ruhr. The Nazis made him a martyr and held nationwide rallies on the day of his death, May 23.

herded the Brownshirts through a period of explosive growth. In the first year of the Nazi takeover, membership had soared from 400,000 to roughly three million. Much of this growth occurred because the SA had absorbed the Stahlhelm and other paramilitary groups under a plan, authorized by Hitler, to create a reserve military force. In addition, so many former members of the outlawed Communist party had joined the Storm Troopers' ranks that Berliners joked, "The SA is like a beefsteak—brown on the outside, red inside." And as their numbers swelled, the Brownshirts threatened to become a law unto themselves. They intervened in the affairs of local government, blackmailed business people, and even claimed jurisdiction in criminal matters.

Hitler had no use for a second revolution. He was a pragmatist, not a socialist, and he wanted to get on with the business of rebuilding Germany's economic and military might. For this goal, and for his long-range aim of German expansion abroad, he needed the cooperation of established institutions such as big business and the army. The revolutionary ardor of the SA had served him well, but now it threatened to alienate those institutions and disrupt his plans.

The Führer tried various tactics to tame Röhm and the Storm Troopers. First came the warnings. As early as July of 1933, Hitler formally proclaimed the end of revolution and called for evolution in its stead. He threatened, "I will suppress every attempt to disturb the existing order as ruthlessly as I will deal with the so-called second revolution, which would lead only to chaos." Next he undercut the Brownshirts in Prussia by ordering Göring both to disband the auxiliary police units formed the previous February and to break up the unauthorized concentration camps that Röhm had established to handle the overflow of prisoners.

Hitler then tried placating Röhm. He appointed him to the cabinet as a minister without portfolio and sent him a cordial letter on New Year's Day 1934, thanking his chief Storm Trooper "for the imperishable services you have rendered." At the same time, however, Hitler hedged his bet. He called in Rudolf Diels, chief of the newly formed Prussian secret police known as the Gestapo, and asked him to gather incriminating information on SA terrorism and on "Herr Röhm and his friendships." In private, the Führer discussed cutting the SA's swollen membership.

It was a good thing, for early in February—a few days after Hitler's first anniversary as chancellor—the SA leader flaunted the military ambitions that worried the Führer even more than Röhm's call for a second revolution. Röhm proposed to the cabinet that the SA become the foundation for an expansion of the Reichswehr into a "people's army" controlled by a single cabinet minister—presumably himself. Here was Röhm's old idea that "the gray rock must be drowned by the brown tide." The notion had long since been rejected by Hitler, but it sent shock waves of apprehension and resentment through the Reichswehr's officer corps.

Hitler could not afford trouble with the army. He needed the generals' expertise to rearm Germany, and he depended upon their loyalty to keep him in power. With the possible exception of his own SA, only the army possessed the strength to depose him. He courted the generals shamelessly, refrained from meddling in promotions and other internal affairs, and secretly agreed to triple the size of the Reichswehr, which was limited to 100,000 men by the Treaty of Versailles.

Under pressure from the generals to put Röhm in his place, Hitler called a top-level meeting for the morning of February 28. Speaking to the assembled commanders of the Reichswehr and the leaders of the SA, he made clear their roles. The Reichswehr would do Germany's fighting; the SA would help defend the nation's borders and give prospective soldiers preliminary military training disguised as sport, but would otherwise confine itself to internal political matters.

For the moment, Röhm appeared to take the setback in stride. At the conclusion of the meeting, he and Defense Minister Werner von Blomberg signed an agreement formalizing Hitler's terms. Röhm then invited everyone present to what he called a "reconciliation breakfast." Not until after Hitler and the generals had left did Röhm bitterly vent his spleen. Declaring that he "had no intention of keeping the agreement," he referred to Hitler as an "ignorant corporal" and called him "disloyal and badly in need of a vacation." To at least one shocked listener, Viktor Lutze, a Röhm subordinate, this intemperate language smacked of treason, and he presently gave a full report to Hitler.

The Führer was reluctant to move, however, and he waited while the tensions mounted. Röhm acted with increasing defiance. He added to the Storm Troopers' stockpile of arms, stepped up military training, staged huge parades, and even established his own foreign office, which held press conferences and gave elaborate banquets for diplomats. The Reichswehr, meanwhile, heightened the contrast by cultivating its relationship with Hitler. Blomberg introduced Nazi indoctrination into army training and published an article that extravagantly praised the chancellor on April 20, Hitler's forty-fifth birthday. The defense minister also flattered the former corporal by renaming in his honor the barracks in Munich that housed Hitler's old outfit, the List Regiment.

In the waning days of spring, tensions peaked. Speaking at Marburg University on June 17, Vice Chancellor Papen, hitherto a yes-man in the cabinet, delivered an uncharacteristically forceful attack on Nazi radicalism and urged Hitler to break with those who advocated a second revolution. "Have we gone through an anti-Marxist revolution," he asked, "in order to carry out a Marxist program?" The vice chancellor's speech, which embodied many of the nation's anxieties, created such a stir that Goebbels banned its publication.

Hitler was furious and ranted to his associates about that "worm" and "ridiculous pygmy" Papen. All the same, he feared that Papen's speech might herald the resurgence of a conservative coalition that would include the president and the generals. Four days after the speech, Hitler flew to Hindenburg's estate in East Prussia. The president lay deathly ill with a prostate ailment. When the Nazi party leader arrived, he learned from Blomberg—and, in a brief audience, from Hindenburg himself—that the president was prepared to declare martial law and put the army in charge if the government could not control Röhm. The prospect of losing the army's allegiance forced Hitler's hand. Now that Hindenburg appeared to be so near death, the Führer needed the army more than ever, because he intended to boldly abolish the presidency and assume its functions as soon as the old man was gone.

If Hitler required further incentive to move against Röhm, it was provided by two of the SA leader's principal rivals within the party. Heinrich Himmler and Hermann Göring, head of the SS and deputy director of the Gestapo, respectively, were so eager to get Röhm out of the way that they fabricated reports of an imminent putsch by him. Hitler may or may not have believed their fictions; Röhm's loose talk and aggressive behavior were evidence enough that he could not be trusted. Hitler seized upon the rumors as a pretext for settling accounts. He ordered Göring and Himmler to launch what came to be known as the Blood Purge, or the Night of the Long Knives.

The purge began in the early hours of Friday, June 30. Hitler himself flew to Bavaria and, accompanied by armed police, arrested Röhm and his top associates at gunpoint at a hotel in Bad Wiessee. All over Germany that morning, execution squads from the Gestapo and SS set to work. Methodically, mostly with guns but occasionally with knives and other weapons, they eradicated much of the SA's leadership and then extended their reach to avenge old Nazi wrongs. Among the several hundred victims were such diverse figures as Gustav von Kahr, who had suppressed the Beer Hall Putsch in 1923; Edgar Jung, the author of Papen's June 17 speech; Gregor Strasser, Hitler's longtime Nazi colleague; and General Kurt von Schleicher, the former chancellor.

The orgy of killing was practically over by Sunday afternoon, July 1, when Hitler hosted a tea party in the gardens of the chancellery. Nazi leaders and cabinet members attended with their wives and children. Hitler amicably mingled with the crowd. Sipping tea, he exchanged social pleasantries with the adults and greeted the children with avuncular affection. Sometime that afternoon, he excused himself from the party long enough to order the execution of his friend turned nemesis, Ernst Röhm, who was being incarcerated in a cell in Munich.

It was a measure of Hitler's power—and of the collective relief at being rid of Röhm's revolutionary menace—that important voices in Germany were raised not in shocked protest, but in praise. On that same July 1, in an official order of the day, Blomberg publicly thanked Hitler for the purge in the name of the army. The next day, while Göring was ordering his police to burn all documents related to the purge, Hindenburg telegraphed his gratitude that Hitler had "nipped all the treasonable intrigues in the bud." On July 3, the cabinet approved a measure legalizing the measures taken "as acts of self-defense by the state."

In the last days of June 1934, Ernst Röhm (right) strolls with a companion in the Bavarian resort of Bad Wiessee, where the SA chieftain was taking a cure for rheumatism.

Hitler himself waited until July 13, then went before the assembled Reichstag in order to explain his actions. He revealed details of the alleged plot involving Röhm, reassured the army that it would be the "sole bearer of arms," and offered this remarkable justification: "If anyone reproaches me and asks why I did not turn to the regular courts of justice for conviction of the offenders, then all I can say to him is this: In this hour, I was responsible for the fate of the German people, and thereby I became the supreme judge of the German people."

Supreme judge and executioner, Hitler could now get on with the process of seizing absolute power. The opportunity presented itself less than three weeks later, on August 2, when President Paul von Hindenburg died, only two months short of his eighty-seventh birthday. Refusing to lie on anything more comfortable than a Spartan iron bed, the old soldier expired with a Bible in his hands and the words "My kaiser, my fatherland!" on his lips.

Hitler was ready. The previous day he had flown to the president's bedside, then hurried back to Berlin in order to convene a night session of the cabinet. Hours before Hindenburg's death, the cabinet had approved

Röhm and a few SA colleagues were staying in this hotel, on the shore of the Tegernsee, when Hitler staged an early-morning raid on June 30 and arrested them for treason.

a law merging the offices of president and chancellor and transferring to Hitler the authority of both offices. Papen had not been present, but the Führer had obligingly affixed the vice chancellor's signature to the new law, which blatantly contravened the Enabling Act's prohibition against tampering with the office of the presidency.

Not content to rest on the cabinet's unanimous approval of the law—or on the new oath of unconditional obedience that every German soldier and sailor had sworn to him almost immediately—Hitler called for a plebiscite on August 19. Again, voting was mandatory. Large lapel pins were distributed to everyone who cast a ballot so that party enforcers could identify anyone who had failed to participate. Citizens who did not display a pin were forcibly taken to the polling places. According to the Nazi-controlled count, nearly nine of every ten Germans formally voted their approval of Hitler as the all-powerful Führer and Reich chancellor. Fewer than 5 million of the nearly 44 million voters dared to say no to Adolf Hitler. The German Reich was now his to lead. ✚

Army and navy officers stand vigil over Hindenburg, who lies in state on his deathbed. Germans of every station mourned the

Seizing the Torch of State

When Paul von Hindenburg died at Neudeck, his estate in East Prussia, on August 2, 1934, Chancellor Hitler was quick to assume the late president's powers as both head of state and military commander in chief. Yet Hitler shrewdly calculated that more than a decree was needed to dramatize his claim to Hindenburg's legacy. Although the legendary field marshal and statesman had asked to be buried in a simple ceremony at Neudeck, the chancellor decided otherwise. The rite would be celebrated sixty-five miles away at the village of Tannenberg, the site of Hindenburg's greatest military triumph, and the Führer would appear in person in order to deliver the eulogy and to symbolically seize the fallen torch.

Hindenburg had won the lasting devotion of his countrymen in 1914, when he answered a summons from retirement to command Germany's Eighth Army against the invading Russians. As fate would have it, he made his stand at Tannenberg, where five centuries earlier Germany's vaunted Teutonic Knights had been crushed by an army of Poles and Lithuanians. Soldiers under Hindenburg's command redeemed that infamous defeat, annihilating a Russian army in a four-day battle. Germans cherished the memory of the victory at Tannenberg throughout the bitter years that were to follow, and during Hindenburg's presidency his admirers erected a glowering, fortresslike monument on the battle site.

Within that somber pile, five days after Hindenburg's death, Hitler delivered his funeral oration to 6,000 assembled military and civilian mourners. Ignoring the fact that Hindenburg had advocated the restoration of a constitutional monarchy, Hitler portrayed the hero of Tannenberg as a true champion of the Nazi uprising. "As Reich president, the field marshal became protector of the National Socialist revolution and therewith of the regeneration of our people," Hitler declaimed. At one point in the ceremony, Hindenburg's grandchildren obligingly offered Hitler the Nazi salute, a tribute that Hindenburg himself had never tendered. And as the patriarch of the old army was laid to rest, the band struck a final ironic note by playing a hymn to one of Hitler's martyred irregulars—Horst Wessel.

Soldiers wearing a new insignia —the Nazi eagle—enter Tannen-berg by torchlight alongside Hindenburg's coffin, which is draped with the imperial flag and crowned with the field marshal's spiked helmet.

A military escort waits outside Neudeck, Hindenburg's ancestral home, to conduct the coffin to Tannenberg. Grateful Germans had refurbished the estate after it slipped from the family's hands following World War I.

At left, troops, veiled mourners, and bareheaded dignitaries surround Hindenburg's catafalque in the courtyard of the Tannenberg monument. Among those presiding was the last surviving field marshal of the imperial army, August von Mackensen, who came forward in Prussian blue to lay a wreath (above). The Lutheran chaplain general commended Hindenburg "to the grace of God," but Hitler added a Wagnerian farewell: "Departed general, enter now into Valhalla!"

Hitler strides past a navy honor guard at the funeral, followed by SS chief Heinrich Himmler *(far left)* and other aides. With studied

simplicity, the Führer wore a plain brown uniform with no insignia as he claimed Hindenburg's mantle as supreme commander.

Acknowledgments

The editors thank the following individuals and institutions for their help in the preparation of this book: Federal Republic of Germany: Berlin—Janos Frecot, Berlinische Galerie; Heidi Klein, Bildarchiv Preussischer Kulturbesitz; Gabrielle Kohler-Gallei, Archiv für Kunst und Geschichte; Wolfgang Streubel, Ullstein Bilderdienst. Hamburg—Heinz Höhne. Hanover—Fritz Tobias. Koblenz—Meinrad Nilges, Bundesarchiv. Munich—Elisabeth Heidt, Süddeutscher Verlag Bilderdienst; Heinrich Hoffmann. Stuttgart—Sabine Oppenländer; Erika Rasthofer, Bibliothek für Zeitgeschichte. German Democratic Republic: Berlin—Hannes Quaschinsky, ADN-Zentralbild; Dr. Jürgen Schebera. Plauen—Walter Ballhause. United States of America: Delaware—Gary Gerber. District of Columbia—Eveline Nave, Library of Congress; Jack Saunders and staff, National Archives.

Picture Credits

Bibliography

Abel, Theodore, *Why Hitler Came into Power*. Cambridge, Mass.: Harvard University Press, 1986.

Allen, William Sheridan:
"The Nazi Rise to Power: A Comprehensible Catastrophe." In *The Rise of the Nazi Regime*. Ed. by Charles S. Maier, Stanley Hoffmann, and Andrew Gould. Boulder, Colo.: Westview, 1986.
The Nazi Seizure of Power. New York: New Viewpoints, 1973.

Angolia, John R., *Cloth Insignia of the NSDAP and SA*. San Jose, Calif.: R. James Bender, 1985.

Bracher, Karl Dietrich:
The German Dictatorship. New York: Praeger, 1970.
"The Technique of the National Socialist Seizure of Power." In *The Road to Dictatorship*. Transl. by Lawrence Wilson. London: Oswald Wolff, 1964.

Bullock, Alan, *Hitler: A Study in Tyranny*. New York: Harper & Row, 1964.

Burden, Hamilton T., *The Nuremberg Party Rallies, 1923-39*. New York: Praeger, 1967.

Childers, Thomas, *The Nazi Voter*. Chapel Hill: University of North Carolina Press, 1984.

Conway, John, transl., *The Path to Dictatorship, 1918-1933*. New York: Praeger, 1967.

Craig, Gordon A.:
Germany, 1866-1945. New York: Oxford University Press, 1978.
The Politics of the Prussian Army, 1640-1945. London: Oxford University Press, 1964.

Davidson, Eugene, *The Making of Adolf Hitler*. New York: Macmillan, 1977.

Diebow, Hans, and Kurt Goeltzer, *Hitler*. Berlin: Verlag Tradition Wilhelm Kolk, 1931.

Dorpalen, Andreas, *Hindenburg and the Weimar Republic*. Princeton, N.J.: Princeton University Press, 1964.

Engelmann, Bernt, *In Hitler's Germany*. New York: Pantheon Books, 1986.

Eyck, Erich, *A History of the Weimar Republic*. Cambridge, Mass.: Harvard University Press, 1963.

Fest, Joachim C., *Hitler*. Transl. by Richard and Clara Winston. New York: Vintage Books, 1975.

Fischer, Conan J.:
"The Occupational Background of the SA's Rank and File Membership during the Depression Years, 1929 to mid-1934." In *The Shaping of the Nazi State*. Ed. by Peter D. Stachura. London: Croom Helm, 1978.
Stormtroopers. London: George Allen & Unwin, 1983.

Flavell, M. Kay, *George Grosz*. New Haven, Conn.: Yale University Press, 1988.

Friedrich, Otto, *Before the Deluge*. New York: Harper & Row, 1972.

Gallo, Max, *The Night of Long Knives*. Transl. by Lily Emmet. New York: Harper & Row, 1972.

Gay, Peter, *Weimar Culture*. New York: Harper & Row, 1970.

Gervasi, Frank, *Adolf Hitler*. New York: Hawthorn Books, 1974.

Goebbels, Joseph, *My Part in Germany's Fight*. Transl. by Kurt Fiedler. New York: Howard Fertig, 1979.

Grunfeld, Frederic V., and the Editors of Time-Life Books, *Berlin* (The Great Cities series). Amsterdam: Time-Life Books, 1977.

Halcomb, Jill, *The SA*. Columbia, S.C.: Crown/Agincourt, 1985.

Halperin, S. William, *Germany Tried Democracy*. New York: W. W. Norton, 1965.

Hamilton, Charles, *Leaders and Personalities of the Third Reich*. San Jose, Calif.: R. James Bender, 1984.

Heiber, Helmut, *Goebbels*. Transl. by John K. Dickinson. New York: Hawthorn Books, 1972.

Hitler, Adolf, *Mein Kampf*. Transl. by Ralph Manheim. Boston: Houghton Mifflin, 1971.

Höhne, Heinz, *The Order of the Death's Head*. Transl. by Richard Barry. New York: Coward-McCann, 1970.

Holborn, Hajo, ed., *Republic to Reich*. Transl. by Ralph Manheim. New York: Pantheon Books, 1972.

Kater, Michael H., *The Nazi Party*. Cambridge, Mass.: Harvard University Press, 1983.

Koch, Karl W. H., *Das Ehrenbuch der SA*. Düsseldorf: Friedrich Floeder Verlag, 1934.

Lane, Barbara Miller, and Leila J. Rupp, transls., *Nazi Ideology before 1933*. Austin: University of Texas Press, 1978.

von Lang, Jochen, *The Secretary*. Transl. by Christa Armstrong and Peter White. New York: Random House, 1979.

Laqueur, Walter, *Weimar: A Cultural History, 1918-1933*. New York: G. P. Putnam's Sons, 1974.

Littlejohn, David, and C. M. Dodkins, *Orders, Decorations, Medals and Badges of the Third Reich*. San Jose, Calif.: R. James Bender, 1968.

Lorant, Stefan, *Sieg Heil!* New York: W. W. Norton, 1974.

MacPherson, Peter, "Lost Glory." *American Photographer*, August 1988.

Manvell, Roger, *Göring*. New York: Ballantine Books, 1972.

Merkl, Peter H., *The Making of a Stormtrooper*. Princeton, N.J.: Princeton University Press, 1980.

Morris, Warren B., Jr., *The Weimar Republic and Nazi Germany*. Chicago: Nelson-Hall 1982.

Mosley, Leonard, *The Reich Marshal*. Garden City, N.Y.: Doubleday, 1974.

Neumann, Franz, *Behemoth*. New York: Harper & Row, 1966.

Noakes, J., and G. Pridham, eds., *The Rise to Power, 1919-1934*. Vol. 1 of *Nazism, 1919-1945*. Exeter, England: University of Exeter, 1983.

Orlow, Dietrich, *The History of the Nazi Party, 1919-1933*. Pittsburgh: University of Pittsburgh Press, 1969.

Pinson, Roppel S., *Modern Germany*. New York: Macmillan, 1966.

Pritchard, R. John, *Reichstag Fire*. New York: Ballantine Books, 1972.

Remak, Joachim, *The Nazi Years*. New York: Simon & Schuster, 1986.

Scholder, Klaus, *The Churches and the Third Reich*. Vol. 1. Philadelphia: Fortress Press, 1988.

Shirer, William L., *The Rise and Fall of the Third Reich*. New York: Simon & Schuster, 1960.

Sington, Derrick, and Arthur Weidenfeld, *The Goebbels Experiment*. New Haven, Conn.: Yale University Press, 1943.

Snyder, Louis L., *Encyclopedia of the Third Reich*. New York: McGraw-Hill, 1976.

Speer, Albert, *Inside the Third Reich*. Transl. by Richard and Clara Winston. New York: Macmillan, 1970.

Stachura, Peter D.:
" 'Der Fall Strasser': Gregor Strasser, Hitler and National Socialism, 1930-1932." In *The Shaping of the Nazi State*. Ed. by Peter D. Stachura. London: Croom Helm, 1978.
Gregor Strasser and the Rise of Nazism. London: George Allen & Unwin, 1983.

Tobias, Fritz, *The Reichstag Fire*. New York: G. P. Putnam's Sons, 1964.

Toland, John:
Adolf Hitler. New York: Ballantine Books, 1977.
Hitler. Garden City, N.Y.: Doubleday, 1978.

Tolstoy, Nikolai, *Night of the Long Knives*. New York: Ballantine Books, 1972.

Turner, Henry Ashby, Jr., *German Big Business and the Rise of Hitler*. New York: Oxford University Press, 1985.

Waite, Robert G. L., *Vanguard of Nazism*. New York: W. W. Norton, 1969.

Wheaton, Eliot Barculo, *Prelude to Calamity: The Nazi Revolution, 1933-35*. Garden City, N.Y.: Doubleday, 1968.

Willett, John, *The Weimar Years*. New York: Abbeville, 1984.

Wilson, Lawrence, transl., *The Road to Dictatorship*. London: Oswald Wolff, 1964.

Wistrich, Robert, *Who's Who in Nazi Germany*. New York: Bonanza Books, 1984.

Wykes, Alan, *The Nuremberg Rallies*. New York: Ballantine Books, 1970.

Index

160; SA at (1933), 160
Proletarian Theater (Berlin): 55
Propaganda: Hitler on, 10-11
Prostitution: in Germany, *45*
Prussia: Communist party suppressed in, 149, 156-157; Göring as governor of, 165, 173; Göring as interior minister of, 148-149, 152, 156, 157-158; government's opposition to Nazi party, 72; government's opposition to SA, 72, 120; Nazi party in state elections, 120-121; Nazis take over police, *148-149;* Papen as Reich commissioner of, 145, 148-149, 165, 169; Social Democratic party suppressed in, 156-157; state government removed, 125-126; state legislature dissolved, 148
Public works: as propaganda, 169-170, 171

R

Raubal, Angela: *88-89*
Raubal, Geli: *88-89;* Hitler's affair with, 88; suicide of, 88, 105
Rauschning, Hermann: on Hitler's villa, 129
Red-Front Fighters' League: 78
Reichsbank: Schacht as president of, 64
Reichspropagandaleitung (RPL): *See* Nazi Party, Reich Propaganda Directorate
Reichstag: 65, 66, 112, *130-131;* approves purge of SA, 176; Brüning in, 161; Catholic Center party in, 161-162; Communist party in, 78, 158, 161, 164, 170; Goebbels in, *80-81;* Hindenburg decrees dissolution of, 129-130; instability of, 73, 74-75, 78, 108, 126; meets at Potsdam (1933), 160-161, *162-163;* meets in Kroll Opera House (1933), 161-164; Nationalist party in, 158, 167; Nazi party in, 10, 12, 39, 68, 78, *80-81,* 112, 121, 126, 129-130, 131, 146, 158, 170, 171; Sender on Nazis in, 80; Social Democratic party in, 78, 158, 161-164; Wels in, 161-162
Reichstag fire (1933): 165, 166; communists and Nazis accused of complicity in, 152-157; set by van der Lubbe, 150-157, *151-155*
Reichswehr: 112; Blomberg as second in command of, 73; distrust of SA, 78-82, 97, 173-174; Eighth Army, 109, 179; fear of revolution, 82; Hitler courts, 174; List Regiment, 174; Nazi indoctrination in, 174; personal loyalty oath to Hitler, 177; at Potsdam (1933), 160; SA attempts to merge with, 173-174; Seeckt as commander of, 87; supports Hindenburg government, 126
Reichswehr, Ministry Bureau of the: 108
Reiter, Mitzi: 20
Rhineland: Allied evacuation of the, 61
Ribbentrop, Joachim von: and Hitler's appointment as chancellor, 135
Röhm, Ernst: 82, 112, *176;* appointed to cabinet, 173; arrested, 175, *177;* at Bad Wiessee, 175, *176, 177;* criticizes Hitler, 172, 174; exiled in Bolivia, *16,* 97; and

formation of SA, 16; as head of SA, 27, 80, 91, 94, 97, 103, 172-174; murder of, 176; supports "second revolution," 172-173
Rosenberg, Alfred: as editor of *Völkischer Beobachter,* 116
Royal property: proposed expropriation of, 22-24
Ruhr Valley: France evacuates, 8, 19, 35

S

Sacco and Vanzetti case: 55
Salomon, Erich: *50*
SA *(Sturmabteilung): cover,* 67, 108, 115, *117, 140-142,* 161, *172;* abortive mutiny by (1931), 82; absorbs Stahlhelm, 173; anti-Semitic activities of, *98-99,* 165; arming of, 98, *102-103;* attempts to merge with Reichswehr, 173-174; at Bad Harzburg, 107; banned, 120, 121, *122-123, 124;* Bavarian government's opposition to, 72, 120; Berlin revolt, 76-77; Bicycle Corps, *139;* at Braunschweig, 107; camaraderie in, *92, 94;* commissioned as auxiliary police, 98, *102-103;* communications training, *97;* communists join (1933), 173; Dortmund rally (1933), *138-139;* 88th Regiment, 70; in election of 1930, 78, *79;* in elections of 1932-1933, 101; fights SS (1930), 76; formation of, 11, 91; Gestapo and purge of, 173, 175; gliding training, *95;* Göring and purge of, 175-176; Hitler and control of, 62, 64, 68-72, 76-77, 106, 173-175; insignia of, *71;* lack of discipline in, 69, 72; lack of funds, 76-77; military training of, *90-91, 92, 96-97;* murder of Pietzuch, 127, 129, 131; 158th Regiment, 71; personal loyalty oath to Hitler, 77; Pfeffer von Salomon as head of, 27, 69, 77; police confrontations with, *100-*101; poster, *60;* at Potsdam, 160; protects party speakers, *100-*101; Prussian government's opposition to, 72, 120; purge of, 175-176; purpose of, 68-72, 91, 92; Reichswehr's distrust of, 78-82, 97, 173-174; at religious services, *93;* Röhm and formation of, 16; Röhm as head of, 27, 80, 91, 94, 97, 103, 172-174; Schleicher and, 97, 112, 121; *Sportabteilung* as predecessor of, 91; sports activities, *94-95;* SS and purge of, 175; street battles with Communists (1932), *124-125;* structure of, *70-71;* and suppression of organized labor, 166, *167;* uniforms of, *70;* use of violence by, 27-28, 62, 91, *101,* 108, 120, 149
Schacht, Hjalmar: as president of Reichsbank, 64
Schirach, Baldur von: as head of Hitler Youth, *143*
Schlageter, Albert: execution of, 172
Schleicher, Kurt von: *76;* appointed chancellor, 131; character traits of, 108-112; courts Hitler, 82, 88, 108-112, 121-122, 127-128; courts Strasser, 131-132;

as defense minister, *111;* dismissed as chancellor, 136; friendship with Oskar von Hindenburg, 73, 121; and Groener, 108, 121; and Hindenburg, 73-74, 88-89, 108, 121-122, 131; manipulation of Weimar government, 73-74, 82, 88-89, 108-112, 121-124, 127, 131-133, 135-136; murder of, 175; and Papen, 122-124, 131; and SA, 97, 112, 121
Schlemmer, Oskar: works of, *48, 52-53*
"Second revolution": Röhm supports, 172-173
Seeckt, Hans von: as commander of Reichswehr, 87
Sender, Toni: on Nazis in the Reichstag, 80
Silesia: in the depression, *42-43*
Social Democratic party: 8, 10, 18, 80, 84, 114, 121, 125, 126; in election of 1928, 34; in elections of 1932-1933, 116, 118-*119,* 126, 147, 158; exiled in Prague, 166; and organized labor, 166; outlawed, 167; in the Reichstag, 78, 158, 161-164; suppressed in Prussia, 156-157
Socialism: Gregor and Otto Strasser and, 20-23, 65, 72
Socialist party: 27, 34, 116; in election of 1928, 35
Soviet Union: 22
Sportabteilung: as predecessor of SA, 91
SS *(Schutzstaffel): 140-141,* 161, *164;* anti-Semitic activities of, *98-99;* banned (1932), 120, *124;* commissioned as auxiliary police, *149;* fights SA (1930), 76; Himmler as head of, 175; personal loyalty oath to Hitler, *171;* and purge of SA, 175; and suppression of organized labor, 166
Stahlhelm (Nationalist veterans' organization): 63, 107, 149, 158-*159;* absorbed by SA, 173
Stahlruten (improvised weapons): 125
State party: disbands, 167
Stennes, Walter: and abortive SA mutiny (1931), 82
Storm Troopers: *See* SA *(Sturmabteilung)*
Strasser, Gregor: 76, 82, 112, 115; at Bamberg party meeting (1926), 23-24; as chief political organizer, 34, 65, 72; on the depression, 83; Goebbels as ally of, 20-22, 24; Goebbels on, 24; at Hanover party meeting (1925), 22-23; on Hitler, 88; as Hitler's rival, 16-*17,* 20, 21-24, 27-28, 34, 65, 72-73, 132-133; murder of, 175; resigns party post, 133; Schleicher courts, 131-132; and socialism, 20-23, 65, 72-73
Strasser, Otto: 65; purged from party, 73, 75, 80; rift with Hitler, 72-73; and socialism, 72-73
Streicher, Julius: 165
Stresemann, Gustav: 8, 19, *21, 35,* 61-62, 64; awarded Nobel Peace Prize, 35, 61; death of, 62